Rev. Dr. Don L. Davis

THE

SIAFU

NETWORK

GUIDEBOOK

Standing Together for Christ

SECOND EDITION

The Urban Ministry Institute, *a ministry of* World Impact, Inc.

The SIAFU Network Guidebook: Standing Together for Christ

The Urban Ministry Institute
3701 E. 13th Street
Wichita, KS 67208

ISBN: 978-1-62932-700-6

Published by TUMI Press
A division of World Impact, Inc.

The Urban Ministry Institute is a ministry of World Impact, Inc.

This *SIAFU Network Guidebook* is in memory of

REV. FRED STOESZ

a dear friend, fellow missionary,
and true warrior of Christ and his Kingdom,
who raised and led his dear family with his wife, Jolene,
for decades in the mean streets of urban America,
who lived his entire life with a white-hot passion
for the Church of Jesus Christ,
and embodied his whole life long
a deep conviction regarding the Holy Spirit's power
to raise up an army of qualified spiritual laborers
among the poorest of the poor.

※ ※ ※ ※ ※ ※ ※

The least one shall become a clan,
and the smallest one a mighty nation;
I am the LORD; in its time I will hasten it.

~ Isaiah 60.22 (ESV)

TABLE OF CONTENTS

PART II
MAKING THE CASE:
WHY YOU NEED A SIAFU CHAPTER IN YOUR CHURCH

PART III
FORMING A COMPANY:
THE HOW-TO'S OF STARTING YOUR SIAFU CHAPTER

APPENDIX

And I looked and arose and said to the nobles and to the officials and to the rest of the people, "Do not be afraid of them. Remember the Lord, who is great and awesome, and fight for your brothers, your sons, your daughters, your wives, and your homes."

~ Nehemiah 4.14

All these, men of war, arrayed in battle order, came to Hebron with a whole heart to make David king over all Israel. Likewise, all the rest of Israel were of a single mind to make David king.

~ 1 Chronicles 12.38

THE SIAFU CHANT

We're unashamed (Without a tear)
We're unafraid (Without a fear)
We'll never quit (We holdin' ground)
We gonna stay (We hangin' 'round!)
All for one (And one for all)
We're for the King (And for the call)
We hold the faith (We go before)
We shout and sing (We makin' war!)

Chorus
Here we are, (We can't be dissed)
Here we be, (We won't be missed)
Here we march, (We settin' out)
Here we speak, (We all shout)
Here we fight, (We throwin' down)
Here we roll, (Around town)
Here we glide, (We on the move)
Here we go, (SIAFU!)

Honor bound (To do the right)
Right on time (To stand and fight)
We stick around (In unity)
We seek to find (To set them free)
We fight to win (To liberate)
We can't be beat (We dedicate)
We're going in (On full attack)
We won't retreat (We'll take it back!)

Chorus

End
Here we are, SIAFU! Here we are, SIAFU!
Here we are, SIAFU! Here we are, SIAFU!
SIAFU!

POWERFUL IN BATTLE FOR THE LORD

(We are) powerful in battle, the soldiers of the Lord
Trained to fight the enemy with the weapons of this war
With a singleness of purpose, be courageous to the core
Just hold your ground, and stand in one accord,
Let's be powerful in battle for the Lord.

Enlist yourselves for battle, flee the petty dreams
Refuse to be distracted by the devil's evil schemes
Surrender, give allegiance unto the risen King
And all your best and brightest gifts unto the altar bring.

And like a mighty army, we've gathered here to fight
Committed to the Savior all, we're standing for the right
And yielded to the Captain, be armed with truth and light
Come strap his heav'nly armor on, be strengthened with his might.

Attention, mighty warriors, come, and stand your ground
Arm yourselves for battle now, and hear the trumpet sound
Stir yourselves like lions, and roar the battle cry
Engage the foe in Jesus' name, and put them all to flight!

We are soldiers of the light, warriors of Jesus Christ.

PREFACE

We dedicated this work to our dear friend and brother, Fred Stoesz, who went to be with the Lord in March 2013. Fred gave the last forty years of his life to a single idea, to an overwhelming passion and dream – to advance the Kingdom of God among the poorest of the poor in the cities of America and the world. An urban missionary, a prayer warrior, a great preacher, and a feisty church planter, Fred's whole life was anchored in a set of convictions which all revolved around his commitment to the poor. Fred's characteristic conviction was simple and absolutely powerful: *God can do anything he wants, through anyone he chooses to accomplish it, and he usually chooses those least likely to be selected by others to do it!*

We were reminded of Fred's insight and burden for city folk when we were drafting these documents, a passion which over many years was demonstrated through his own evangelism, preaching, discipling, and church planting. *The Urban Ministry Institute*, which this year recognizes its eighteenth year of existence, mirrors Fred's passion and vision. We believe that revival for the world will come from those given the least chance to do it. It will not be from the ranks of the educated, the wealthy, the sophisticated, and the well known that God will accomplish his greatest feats and works in the cities of the world. Rather, God has chosen the poor to be rich in faith, to be the very heirs of the Kingdom who will bring great glory and honor to his name (James 2.5)!

This work is a tribute to men like Fred, who, though from a suburban neighborhood in Canada that looked nothing like the tough streets he would raise his family in, still believed in the power of the Holy Spirit to transform the city from the bottom up, from the poor upwards. Like water, the grace of God always trickles to the lowest point, and there, begins to rise. Truly, as our Lord declared, it will be the meek who inherit the earth (Ps. 37.11; Matt. 5.5). Our God is the God who does not see as people see, who look on the appearance. Rather, our God looks on the heart (1 Sam. 16.9).

The mission of the SIAFU (pronounced *see-AH-foo*) Network is to establish a viable, effective network of urban Christian men and women whose goal is to inspire each other to take full responsibility for one another's lives and well-being. As soldiers of Christ, urban Christians must stand up for our marriages and families, for our churches and congregations, and for our communities to advance the Kingdom of Christ in the city.

Why is SIAFU needed? It is necessary because we must find new ways to assemble together in order to empower one another to befriend and mentor each other to reach unchurched family members and friends with the Gospel. Furthermore, we can use these gatherings to disciple new Christians to live the Christian life, and to challenge one another to serve as faithful stewards and servants in our respective Christian churches. A local assembly is an outpost of the Kingdom, wherever the Lord may have placed that church. Through SIAFU, we hope to work together as churches and disciples in order to identify, train, and release godly, spiritually qualified laborers who can start new ministries, plant healthy churches, and reach lost urban neighborhoods for Christ.

As you ponder the arguments and applications set forth in this guidebook, it would be helpful for you to keep in mind the principle of reversal. Simply stated, it testifies that in the Kingdom of God, everything is upside-down to how it is viewed and signified in the world. The ethic of the Kingdom requires that you understand life from a new perspective, from God's vantage point, as it were, and comprehend the possibilities for change and transformation through his eyes, and not your own.

This book makes a case that mobilizing urban disciples is the only way that the cities of the world can possibly be evangelized and transformed. They and they alone must rise to the occasion and respond to the grace of God with surrender and passion to see God do new things in the city.

This is not a novel idea; rather, this principle of God working with the least and lowly is well documented in Scripture. For instance, the Word declares that it is the poor who shall become rich, and the rich shall become poor (Luke 6.20-26), and the law breaker and the undeserving will be saved (Matt. 21.31-32). Those who humble themselves shall be exalted (1 Pet. 5.5-6), and those who exalt themselves shall be brought low (Luke 18.14). It is the blind who will be given sight (John 9.39), and those who claim to see here and now shall be made blind (John 9.40-41). God has chosen what is foolish in the world to shame the wise, what is weak in the world to shame the strong, and what is low and despised to bring to nothing things that are (1 Cor. 1.27-28).

Without a doubt, only God can produce a revival to transform the city, and if he chooses to, the most likely candidates to lead that movement will be those most neglected and forgotten in the city itself. As they say here in the city, this is the way God "rolls."

According to the Bible, God has determined to fight against the spiritual forces of evil that have plagued humankind since the beginning of time. The prophets and apostles assert that the LORD sent his Son, Jesus Christ, to come to earth to win final victory over all the principalities and powers that have threatened to overthrow his good will and harm his creation. In the final judgment, all will be made right, under God's reign. Until then, believers are to represent God's interests, advancing his Kingdom in all places. All citations through this SIAFU Guidebook that speak of battle, warfare, and enemies relate to this spiritual warfare, this intent of God to put evil down and make all things new, under his reign.

> According to the Bible, God has determined to fight against the spiritual forces of evil that have plagued humankind since the beginning of time.

No mention of battle or fighting within this book relates to harming people or property, hurting any person in any way, or advocating that anyone be treated with less than full respect, regardless of their beliefs. As the apostle Paul describes this conflict, we do not fight against "flesh and blood" (human enemies and combatants), but rather against spiritual forces seeking to harm humankind and God's creation. (Eph. 6.10-12 – Finally, be strong in the Lord and in the strength of his might. [11] Put on the whole armor of God, that you may be able to stand against the schemes of the devil. [12] For we do not wrestle against flesh and blood, but against the rulers, against the authorities, against the cosmic powers over this present darkness, against the spiritual forces of evil in the heavenly places.) The call to spiritual battle is not a call to do anyone any harm; rather, it is a call to represent Christ and his kingdom, a call to love God and to love others. (Rom. 13.8-10 – Owe no one anything, except to love each other, for the one who loves another has fulfilled the law. [9] For the commandments, "You shall not commit adultery, You shall not murder, You shall not steal, You shall not covet," and any other commandment, are summed up in this word: "You shall love your neighbor as yourself." [10] Love does no wrong to a neighbor; therefore love is the fulfilling of the law.)

This book is a testament to Fred and to all those who still believe that we gain the next world by losing this one (1 Tim. 6.7), and who think that to love this life is to lose it, and to hate this life is to keep the promise of the life to come (John 12.25). If you are interested in learning how you can practically advance the Kingdom where you live, with others just like you in the neighborhood where you live, read on.

By standing together as one for the sake of the Kingdom in the city, we can prove decisively in our own lives that you truly become the greatest by being the servant of all (Mark 10.42-45). Only God can raise up a generation among the least lovely and most unlikely to transform our neighborhoods for Christ. May it ever be!

So, please, continue to read on, dear friend, and join this amazing movement of the Lord that recognizes and responds to the calling forth of an army of urban disciples to take our cities for God!

Don L. Davis
April 1, 2013

DISCLAIMER REGARDING WORLD IMPACT, TUMI, AND OUR SIAFU CHAPTERS

Each SIAFU chapter functions under its own authority and autonomy. Neither TUMI nor World Impact (TUMI's parent organization) are responsible for and will accept no liability connected to the actions of any specific SIAFU chapters or members. This means that TUMI and World Impact are not responsible for the finances or debt of any chapters or members. Also, we are not responsible for direct, indirect, incidental or consequential damages resulting from any SIAFU chapter's efforts or involvement.

We count our chapters as limited partners, and thus nothing in our agreement will create any joint venture, agency, franchise, sales representative, or employment relationship between us the parties, without our express permission. No SIAFU chapter will have any authority to make or accept any offers or representations on our behalf. In becoming a SIAFU Chapter, you will pledge, therefore, not to make any statement, whether on your site or otherwise, that in any way represents itself as an official World Impact/TUMI statement.

Finally, no warranty is established, expressed, or implied in your forming a SIAFU Chapter. Each SIAFU Chapter is a specific, particular, and independent entity, and therefore responsible for its own activities. We are not and will not be held responsible for any debts, actions, damages, or failures, either tangible or intangible, resulting from your involvement with SIAFU.

While these commitments are clear for us, we emphasize these guidelines both for our mutual protection and freedom to experiment as partners. Each SIAFU Chapter is empowered and free to pursue its own goals in sync with the guidelines of the SIAFU Network. TUMI and World Impact want you to succeed in every way in your efforts, and to feel the freedom to pursue those dreams and goals God lays on your heart for your church and community. We will do all we can to aid you, creating resources and hosting events to that end.

STANDING TOGETHER FOR CHRIST INSIDE THE WALLS
SIAFU IN PRISONS AND JAILS

OUR VISION

At The Urban Ministry Institute (TUMI), we have a strong vision to equip men and women to return to society upon release from prison and jail. The best way to facilitate the process of re-entry is to establish a network of friends and family who are ready to walk with men and women when they are released. This must be done the first hour, the first day, the first week, and the first month after they walk out the gate.

The second important factor is to create a strong sense of identity and belonging for men and women, while they are still incarcerated. Everyone needs to belong. SIAFU creates an identity for the incarcerated that can be carried forward when they are released. SIAFU chapters create a bridge of godly identity where the formerly incarcerated belong to something that transcends prison/jail.

The link between incarceration and re-entry can be served by local churches or ministries on the outside. Volunteers from these churches or organizations can sponsor and oversee SIAFU chapter gatherings functioning on the inside. And, after these prisoners have been released, the sponsoring church or ministry may welcome these ex-offenders into their chapter on the outside. We are convinced that these SIAFU sponsoring churches and ministries can provide long-term stability and service to institutions where rapid turnover occurs constantly, among inmate populations, chaplains, and officials.

DISCLAIMERS

This SIAFU guidebook was written primarily for churches on *the outside*, but this fact in no way shuts out or ignores the need of the incarcerated for the kind of belonging that a SIAFU Chapter can provide. However, because of the official regulations of prisons and jails (with their particular policy limitations), how you apply and use the guidebook's protocols will need to be modified in order to conform to each prison and jail's requirements.

Therefore, all references to leadership positions (offices) of a Chapter, handling of finances, references to membership, service projects, collecting of contact information (email, mailing address, or phone number), or other problematic issues only refer to the function of the Chapter on the outside, whether to volunteers or to those given authority by the institution.

Everything listed in this guidebook should be interpreted and applied so as to comply with and obey the official policies of a participating prison or jail. This means that every SIAFU Chapter must comply with the normal rules that govern the Department of Corrections in the state it is in.

For instance, SIAFU Chapters on the inside will not be able to use the leadership offices or require strict membership compliance as in a Chapter's normal operation. Essentially chapters on the inside will need to function more as a Christian "call out" within the prison or jail, a gathering that is sponsored by a particular church or ministry. This will provide both an opportunity to encourage our Christian brothers and sisters who are in the facility as well as share our testimonies of faith with those who attend who may not yet know Christ. *Under no circumstances can any church- or ministry-sponsored SIAFU chapter change, overrule, or ignore the formal policies of the correctional facility they exist in.* Chapters on the inside must function under the jurisdiction and oversight of the correctional system which has allowed them to host such a gathering in their facility.

Within this guidebook, you will observe specific note sections addressing how a point under discussion relates to those sponsoring a SIAFU Chapter within correctional facility. Those notes will be titled "For Chapters on the Inside." We designed these notes to clarify specific issues and navigate correctional policy as you strive to host a successful chapter within the prison or jail you serve.

We recognize that the church on the inside can be as robust as any church on the outside, and in fact, most churches on the inside provide a healthier brotherhood/sisterhood than any churches in the world. In fact, some of the cause of recidivism is due to the lack of strong Christian community on the outside. Therefore, nothing in this Guidebook is meant to diminish the ability of the church on the inside to carry out their responsibilities before Christ.

EXAMPLES

The service projects in this Guidebook are targeted to the context of the church on the outside. The following are some examples of service projects that could be considered on the inside:

1. Sermons
2. Bible study leader
3. Prayer requests or meetings
4. Recreational evangelistic events

GLOSSARY OF TERMS

For those who are not familiar with ministry to the incarcerated, the following is a brief list of commonly used terms.

1. Recidivism – repeated or habitual relapse, as into crime
2. Shank – a homemade knife/weapon; made out of scrap of metal, even chicken bones found anywhere and sharpened like a knife and bottom tightly wrapped with a cloth as a handle
3. SHU – special housing unit, usually isolation unit in maximum security prison, typically in lockdown 23 out of 24 hours per day

DOS AND DON'TS

1. Carefully follow all the rules and protocols of each institution.

2. Don't give any personal contact information to inmates. Always use the contact information of the church only, po box if possible.

3. Contact with family members of inmates through the mail, phone, email or person contact is not allowed.

4. Embracing, hugging or kissing an inmate is not permitted.

5. Follow all directions given by the security/correctional staff.

If you intend to extend your SIAFU chapter into a jail or prison, please indicate in your application. If you decide to extend your chapter to a jail or prison at a later date, please notify the SIAFU Director so we can conduct proper communication with you about resources as they develop.

Welcoming Brothers and Sisters Home
Ex-Offenders and Your SIAFU Chapter

At the very heart of the SIAFU Network's mission is a deep passion that urban folk, those whom the Lord has redeemed and transformed, will be used of the Lord to win the city. Those considered both unlovely and unlikely will be those whom God equips to be used of him to advance his Kingdom! Our desire and purpose with the Network is to help mobilize urban churches to equip urbanites – men, women, boys, and girls – to serve Christ in the city. Through the power of the Holy Spirit, they can get this done!

The Urban Ministry Institute (TUMI) and Prison Fellowship have partnered together and have established TUMI Satellites in prisons around the country. Over time, hundreds of ex-offenders will be released from prison having been equipped with TUMI's seminary-level training. All of these unique and dear brothers (and sisters!) in Christ will certainly need a church home when they are paroled or serve their sentence. Each one will need the kind of welcome and acceptance deserving of any disciple of Christ, and will need the pastoral care and personal mentoring and friendship that will help them discover and use their gifts for Christ. Each one will need to be integrated into a healthy, functioning assembly of believers where they can be known, loved, and where they can serve and grow with others who love the Lord Jesus.

We are convinced that our SIAFU Chapters can be that kind of welcoming, empowering community for these dear men and women. Our intent is to receive information from Prison Fellowship regarding the parole and release of our TUMI students, and we will seek to share their release information with churches hosting SIAFU Chapters in their area. Our SIAFU Chapters can become welcoming centers, the kind of places that receive these dear disciples of Jesus without suspicion or shame. Our Chapters can be the kind of places that incorporate them into a Christian fellowship, making their transition into the church and society more smoothly, and in a way that honors God.

Ultimately, our goal is simple for all the ex-offenders in our TUMI student community. We are trusting God that every last one of these believers will be incorporated into a loving church, where they will be welcomed and accepted as full-fledged members of the body of Christ. The SIAFU Chapter can be a smooth, simple, and effective means by which we bring ex-offenders into Christian community in a local church.

Your Chapter, by definition, can facilitate this kind of "incorporation" of these ex-offenders through its key goals and objectives. Every SIAFU Chapter seeks to:

- *Befriend urban disciples among one another:* Ex-offenders, who do not know anyone, can attend our SIAFU gatherings, form new, healthy relationships, and learn how to walk as friends with other believers, as well as learn how to befriend others.

- *Encourage urban disciples to edify one another:* In our SIAFU Chapters, ex-offenders can be encouraged and strengthened by their fellow members in a group anchored in a local church, submitted to pastoral authority. They can be lifted up, protected from harm as they participate in the gatherings, studies, prayer times, fellowship, and service to others sponsored by your Chapter.

- *Challenge urban disciples to serve as ambassadors of Christ:* These dear men and women will also learn how to serve and use their gifts for the benefit of others. Through your Chapter's service projects, they can be challenged to be hospitable, generous, and sacrificial, employing their talents and resources to meet the needs of others in the community.

So then, the very goals of a SIAFU Chapter can make it much easier to welcome ex-offenders and integrate them into the life of healthy Christian community. We must welcome them into our midst, accepting them as full disciples, and expect them to live holy, godly, and commendable lives through the power of the Spirit. This is the power of the Gospel, and should be the DNA of every SIAFU Chapter. Our motto must be "We welcome all who receive the Master, and we turn no one away who commits their life to him. We will leave no man (or woman) behind!" God can use your Chapter to be a haven of rest to anyone seeking to find the Savior, anyone desiring to turn their life around in absolute surrender to him. Through God's grace, we can bring them into our fellowship and protect them, keeping them in as members of Christ's body – and our SIAFU Chapters.

Let us learn, then, to be open to how God may choose to use our particular SIAFU Chapter to welcome and incorporate ex-offenders into our fellowship. Remember, this entire movement is about the Holy Spirit energizing urban folk to transform the city. Christ is building an army and we are calling urban folk to join that army. We can only take back our families, our streets, and our neighborhoods if we welcome the servants of Jesus he has called to do that work. They will be the very ones to do it, perhaps the only ones who can.

Our God is God, and he shows no respect of persons – and neither should we. God can use anyone he wants to for whatever purpose he chooses – whether that person is a young momma, an aged grandpa, a suburban college graduate, an urban high school dropout, or a newly paroled ex-offender. God raises folk up for his own purpose and uses them for what he has called them to be. Let this be our heart, our conviction, and our commitment.

Stay tuned to our national website to see developments on how our SIAFU Chapters are becoming the kind of welcome centers for ex-offenders that please God and disciple future leaders for the city!

INTRODUCTION
WELCOME TO THE MOTHER OF ALL BATTLES, THE CAMPAIGN OF OUR TIME

> Listen, my beloved brothers, has not God chosen those who are poor in the world to be rich in faith and heirs of the kingdom, which he has promised to those who love him?
>
> ~ James 2.5

If you are an urban Christian, you are caught up in a great battle, a single conflict which is part of a larger war. Yes, the universe is at war, with everything in creation at stake. The opposing forces are disciplined and committed, and in the end, there can only be a single victor. Believe it or not, understand it or ignore it, you still have a role in one of the greatest spiritual struggles in the history of humankind. With hundreds of millions of souls in play, we must each decide whose side we will fight on in this, the campaign of our time.

This motif of spiritual war is prominent throughout the Holy Scriptures, which tell the story of God's commitment to rescue creation from the tyranny of the devil, to save humankind from the penalty and power of sin, and to call together a people from the nations who would belong to him through Christ, his Son. Our God is a man of war (Exod. 15.1-4), a great Lord who promised to send his Son who would be Champion for humankind and all creation, reconciling all things to himself, and establishing his reign in the earth.

We know that Jesus of Nazareth was this promised Champion, who through his incarnation, death, resurrection, ascension, session, and return will accomplish God's rule, including over the dark cities of our time. This basic biblical theology, this faith, is often referred to as the Great Tradition, and TUMI's ongoing passion and project is to recover, articulate, and embody God's truthful Story of redemption and restoration of the world that spans from creation to the consummation of all things. This is key to understanding what God is doing in the world, and central to knowing how we are to live as disciples of Christ in the city today.

The Bible tells the Story of God's determination to restore his kingdom rule, anchored in his loving-kindness and covenantal faithfulness. The Lord God is determined to restore his creation and save out of all humankind a people of his own possession forever. God's Story is authoritatively told in the Scriptures inspired by the Holy Spirit. The same Scriptures which reveal God's kingdom purpose through the covenants to the Patriarchs lay out in detail the history of Israel, the person and work of Jesus Christ, and his Church.

Since the coming of the Holy Spirit, this Story of rescue and restoration has been cherished, celebrated, and guarded by the Church through the ages, the people of God, in whose life and faith the Story continues to be told, enacted, and expressed. In all aspects of our life together – our theology and worship, our spirituality and discipleship, and our service and mission – the Story of God's glory and grace is embodied in us as witness to the world. We are players in the drama of God, a drama that is being acted out in the streets and neighborhoods of America's inner cities.

FACING A GREAT NEED: THE INNER CITIES OF AMERICA

At first glance, the cities of America (and the world) appear to be in trouble, even to be left out of God's drama. Violence, crime, broken families, and despair haunt their streets and neighborhoods, with little hope of change or rescue. Even many Christians have given up, raising the white flag of resignation over the cities of the world, surrendering them to the control of the enemy. Long-term despair and doubt about what God can do in the cities have many believers consigning the cities to the control of the enemy, practically turning those who dwell in them over to those dark forces which prey on the vulnerable and neglected.

Yet, Jesus declared that the gates of hell would not prevail against his church (Matt. 16.18). Our cities can be won, healed, and transformed – all we need is for the brothers and sisters to unite in common purpose for Christ!

The need of the hour for the mean cities of America and the world is clear and plain. We must recruit every godly urban Christian to make themselves available to the Spirit in a new way. As warriors of the Holy Spirit, we must strive with every ounce of our being to mobilize urban disciples into a national community, a common brotherhood and sisterhood who share the same longings, experiences, and dreams as they represent Christ in the cities where they live! Everyone must be mobilized, outfitted, and deployed for service. No one, however young or old, can afford to sit idly on the sidelines during this stark and difficult battle. This is the time for urban churches, urban Christians, and urban leaders to redouble their efforts in the fight, and for everyone, regardless of their status or station in the Church, to report for duty to advance the Kingdom of God. This is the moment of our lives to stand, and to be counted for the Lord!

The SIAFU Network (pronounced *see-AH-foo*) is a practical means to enable urban disciples to stand together for Christ in the city!

FORMING A GREAT ARMY: THE SIAFU NETWORK

OUR MISSION AND PURPOSE
We adopted the siafu ant as our model for the network. The writer of Proverbs spoke of the wisdom and ingenuity of ants who, as they worked together, could accomplish great things for themselves. "Go to the ant, O sluggard; consider her ways, and be wise. Without having any chief, officer, or ruler, she prepares her bread in summer and gathers her food in harvest" (Prov. 6.6-8). Although small and vulnerable as single creatures, they become a mighty and fearsome army when they stand together as one!

> The SIAFU Network is a national association of Chapters anchored in local urban churches, organizations, and/or ministries specifically designed to identify, equip and release spiritually qualified urban servant-leaders to reach and transform the poorest unreached communities in urban America.

The mission of the SIAFU Network is to establish a viable, effective network of urban Christian men and women whose goal is to inspire each other to take full responsibility for one another's lives and well-being, for their marriages and families, for their churches and congregations, and for their communities to advance the Kingdom of Christ in the city.

Our desire is to empower urban Christians to both befriend and mentor one another in order to equip each other to evangelize our unchurched family members and friends, to follow up and disciple new Christians to live the Christian life, and to serve as faithful stewards and servants in our respective Christian churches as outposts of the Kingdom where God has placed them. We also hope to collaborate together in order to identify, train, and release godly, spiritually qualified laborers who can plant churches and help spawn church planting movements which will target the unreached urban neighborhoods of America.

A Brief Overview of the Siafu Ant

The name for this new and exciting collaboration of urban Christians is taken from the example of the African siafu ant community, hailed by the Discovery Channel as the world's fiercest and mightiest social community. A powerful example of community builders, their nests can hold up to twenty-two million members, making them the world's largest social community and easily one of the most productive, inventive, and remarkable groups ever. Siafu are small, vulnerable, and pesky, easily overcome if you attack or seek to destroy one of them isolated and alone, as a mere individual.

However, when banded together in common unity for the single purpose of the survival and strengthening of the community, they are virtually invincible, taking down all kinds of different animals, from goats to buffalo, and (as has sometimes been reported) even elephants in their wake. Their ingenuity and industry (and absolute fierceness) are well known among those who study all the creatures of the insect kingdoms. They are a fitting symbol of the potential that urban Christian men and women possess if they only can unite for the sake of mutual inspiration, edification, equipping, and empowerment. The advancement of the Kingdom of God in America's inner cities lies with urban Christians – identified, inspired, trained, and released for Christ!

One of the great challenges of urban Christians is their sense of isolation and aloneness, their inability to connect with others who share their dreams and struggles. The SIAFU Network intends to learn from the siafu ants, who have mastered the art of living in and for community.

The African Siafu Living the Principle of Networking Community	
As Individuals	As a Community
1 - 15 mm long Blind, tiny, and tender Vulnerable No purpose Intimidated Are a pest Easily stopped	Nest is 20 million strong Mobile networked colony Feared by all Dynamic vision Nobody messes with Consume 2 million pests daily Only stopped by fire Can bring down anything

A small brown speckled frog hops through the leaves of the Riverine Forest floor. It creeps forward for a few seconds and swallows whole a bright green grasshopper that was sitting beside a flower. It hops again, this time misjudged, rubs its face in pain and tries to hop again, lands on its back and is swallowed in a rippling mass of dark red bodies. Ten minutes later, nothing is left of the frog, but the four-inch wide highway of red ants remains. Biting red ants, or "Siafu" in Kiswahili live in colonies, but unlike most ants, do not have a permanent home. The ants range from 1 to 15 mm long, hunt at night, and hide in a hole in the ground or in a tree during the day, They shift locations as the insect, and sometimes frog-like, prey is exhausted. The Riverine Forests of Serengeti, being dark and moist, have Siafu hunting all night long and all day as well. They form either highways as they travel from their lair to the hunting field or fans when they are actively hunting. Siafu hunt by sensing the carbon dioxide that insects and animals breath out. If a person is playful and brave, or just plain stupid, they can tease the Siafu by blowing on the trails of ants and watching them burst into activity, pincers held high, looking for prey. Siafu nests of a few days old are typically a hole in a tree with a thick pile of insect bodies piled up outside the opening. While the bulk of the Siafu's food is insects, they can eat a small animal such as a shrew or a frog if it happens to get caught.

Some people have claimed to see Siafu moving by forming terrifying rolling balls as large as a basketball. In truth, these swarms of Siafu do occur, but they are normally a mass of Siafu surrounding and biting a prey animal, and are seldom more than a few inches across. People claim that these fierce little warriors can climb up inside the trunk of an elephant and bite. It is doubtful that anyone has been close enough to witness this, but when the Siafu are particularly active, such as after a rain storm, you will never find elephants in the same Riverine Forest.

Siafu, though aggressive and painful, are not at all a bad thing, even for people. If you live in Africa and Siafu swarm into your house, they eat all of the other ants, roaches, spiders, and everything else that slithers crawls or creeps, and then they go, leaving you in peace. Peace, that is, as long you have somewhere to stay for a day or two.

~ http://www.serengeti.org/flying_ant.html

How SIAFU Chapters Work

SIAFU is a national association of Chapters anchored in local urban churches and ministries designed to identify, equip, and release spiritually qualified servant leaders to reach and transform the poorest unreached communities in urban America. Chapters are hosted within local churches or related ministries. Since local churches are the outposts of the Kingdom, all SIAFU Chapters are connected to and under the authority* of a local church or ministry.

We have created an elegant, simple structure specifically designed to connect urban believers, both men and women, to come together, to pray, fellowship, and challenge one another to fight for the sake of their churches, families, and communities.

We hope to facilitate their efforts by strengthening the ties and connections among urban churches and Christians through the sponsorships of regional men's and women's conferences, and the establishment of local SIAFU Chapters where urban Christians regularly gather to edify and equip one another through prayer, testimony, worship, teaching, and training. We will facilitate and encourage regional conferences and Chapters to sponsor their own SIAFU workshops, seminars, and training sessions on the specialized needs and interests of their members. God willing, we hope to create over time a lively online presence filled with helpful resources (both hard copy and digital) that will be specially designed to address the particular needs and goals of urban Christians as they seek to advance the Kingdom where they live.

*FOR CHAPTERS ON THE INSIDE

Please remember that although a church or ministry will be sponsoring the SIAFU Chapter on the inside, under no circumstances can any church- or ministry-sponsored SIAFU chapter change, overrule, or ignore the formal policies of the correctional facility they exist in. Chapters on the inside must function under the jurisdiction and oversight of the correctional system which has allowed them to host such a gathering in their facility.

The Driver Ant, Locally Known as 'Siafu' (*Dorylus nigricans*)
Driver ants have the largest colonies of any social insect. When they swarm the effect is so daunting that the whole jungle flees; even elephants are said to run from them. There are at least two castes: workers measure about 0.5 cm in length, and soldiers are almost three times that size. The queen resembles a large ant with

an enormous abdomen. She can be up to 5 cm long. Males are winged and are about 3 cm long.

Driver ants are found throughout the forests of West Africa and the Congo. They inhabit rainforest and savannah, and these ants feed on any animal life in their path! They hunt by swarming. They will dismember up to 100,000 prey animals in a single raid.

Colonies of driver ants can number up to 22 million. Almost daily, swarms embark on raids for food which can be brought back to the nest. Although totally blind, driver ants have no problems getting around. They rely on touch, smell and chemical signals from the abdomen of the leading ants. The swarms can travel at up to 20 meters per hour, stripping all animal life in their path. They are also known to raid the nests of other social insects, although never those of other driver ants. They do not rely on stings to attack; rather they use their large and powerful mandibles to create puncture wounds and tear off sections. Driver ants have a larger impact on their habitat than any other creature and they have to move location at regular intervals to find new feeding grounds. During their nomadic existence they form temporary nests called 'bivouacs' made from the living members of the colony, in which they house the developing grubs. Whenever the ants swarm or migrate, they form large highways of workers, bordered by the soldiers, which hang over the action, their mandibles waving, to protect the colony as it moves.

All of the ants in the colony are female. However, only one of them, the queen, is responsible for breeding. She lays 1-2 million eggs every month, almost continuously. She gets sperm from the bizarre male driver ant – a large winged insect known as the sausage fly. It measures about 3 cm in length, and flies from one colony to another in order to stumble upon an ant highway. Once it does, its wings are removed and it is taken back to the nest where it is used as a sperm donor. The queen driver ant is the largest ant in the world.

~ BBC's Science and Nature
http://www.bbc.co.uk/nature/wildfacts/factfiles/3086.shtml

JOIN THE MOVEMENT:
CONSIDER FORMING A CHAPTER OF THE SIAFU NETWORK

With so much at stake in Christians answering Christ's call to prophesy and demonstrate deliverance to the cities of America, my heart prayer is that you might consider forming a SIAFU Chapter in your local church or Christian organization. Where two or more disciples gather in the name of Christ, there he is in the midst of them (Matt. 18.20). I am convinced that if we were to mobilize urban disciples of Jesus for the honor and glory of Christ, and for the evangelization and transformation of our neighborhoods, Almighty God will visit us. God has shown in numerous historical contexts that, if his people take him seriously, prepare their hearts for a new move of God, and make themselves available to him to do great things, he can bring revival, renewal, and dramatic change to the city.

Amazingly, all the Lord requires to see this change occur is for his people to prepare themselves for his visitation and remember their shared calling and purpose in the Gospel. Who knows what the Father may accomplish through the millions of urban disciples who currently stand unused and neglected in our cities? What could God do if ordinary urban Christians became united and mobilized under a common purpose to see Jesus exalted in every urban neighborhood in America? We could be on the brink of genuine revival. The tip of the spear of that revival will be mobilized, motivated, and transformed urban disciples standing together for Christ in the city!

JOIN THE SIAFU NETWORK IN ORDER TO
WIN THE LOST AND MAKE DISCIPLES

SIAFU activities are specifically designed to help urban disciples bond together in Christ through fellowship, testimony, prayer, and service. Your Chapter will become a strong, central place to bring seeking souls, to identify emerging servant leaders, to equip hungry disciples for effective ministry, and to evangelize the lost and make disciples in their communities where they live.

JOIN THE SIAFU NETWORK IN ORDER TO STRENGTHEN YOUR LOCAL CHURCH

SIAFU is built on a deep conviction and allegiance to local churches, under the authority of local pastors. Through your Chapter you will create a forum to help you identify and equip your leadership pool in your congregation. Your Chapter will enable them to assemble together, befriend one another, and challenge each other to display their love for Christ through service projects.

JOIN THE SIAFU NETWORK IN ORDER TO TOUCH YOUR NEIGHBORHOOD WITH THE LOVE OF CHRIST

Because we affirm that we were created in Christ for good works (Eph. 2.8-10), SIAFU Chapters select ministry projects to serve and care for others, both inside and outside the church, resulting in real transformation in our communities.

This book is designed to enable you to think through the arguments and evidence for the cause of mobilizing urban Christians together for the sake of ministry and mission in the city. Part I, *Assembling God's Warriors: Toward a Strategy to Win the City,* deals with the basic principles and truths that undergird the idea of mobilizing urban disciples for action. Part II, *Making the Case: Why You Need a SIAFU Chapter in Your Church,* poses and refutes the top objections to forming a SIAFU Chapter in a church, answering those objections in the spirit of faith that God has given to those who are the least in this world. Finally, Part III, *Forming a Company: The How-To's of Starting Your SIAFU Chapter,* lays out practically and simply all the steps you'll need to take if you choose to start your own SIAFU Chapter. And, of course, any questions that you fail to get answers to in this meaty little guidebook can be found on our website, *www.tumi.org/siafu,* a one-stop place to get what you need related to the SIAFU Network.

Let us who love the city affirm with all our hearts that God is raising up an army of urban disciples whom he is preparing to mobilize to advance his Kingdom and strengthen his Church. These will undoubtedly be ordinary men and women who love the Lord and their families, who love the Church and the Word, and who look for the return of Christ. God will use common folk who are filled with the Holy Spirit to mobilize an army to declare his praise. Won't you join us, and represent the Kingdom of Jesus with honor, in your neighborhood, where you live? Everything is at stake in you joining this cause. May the Lord lead you as you consider playing your part in the great cosmic drama of our Lord!

FOR CHAPTERS ON THE INSIDE

This is also the case for Chapters inside Prison walls. Chapters on the inside will need to function more as a Christian "call out" within the prison or jail, a gathering that is sponsored by your church or ministry. This will provide both an opportunity to encourage our Christian brothers and sisters who are in the facility as well as share our testimonies of faith with those who attend who may not yet know Christ.

- Your church- or ministry-sponsored SIAFU Chapter will be under the authority of the corrections facility. Although you should be free to minister to and encourage the men or women in your SIAFU Chapter, you have no spiritual authority over them. Continue to encourage, rebuke, exhort, challenge, build up, comfort and teach them but realize that all of their authority is in the corrections system they are a part of.

- Chapters on the inside will not be able to use the leadership offices or require strict membership compliance as in a Chapter's normal operation as it is against the policy of most Departments of Corrections to allow one inmate to have leadership or authority over another.

- There are ideas for service projects that can be done inside prison walls in the section of the book titled: "Standing Together for Christ Inside the Walls: SIAFU in Prisons and Jails."

PART I:
ASSEMBLING
GOD'S WARRIORS
TOWARD A STRATEGY
TO WIN THE CITY

ASSEMBLING GOD'S WARRIORS
TOWARD A STRATEGY TO WIN THE CITY

In order to understand why SIAFU can be important to the urban church and the penetration of the city with the Gospel of Christ, we must grapple with the first truths of the Kingdom as they relate to urban spirituality. We ought never begin a discussion of urban ministry with our own reaction and response to the chaos and need of the city. We should never pretend that who we are and what we think in ourselves can ever serve as the foundation of legitimate kingdom ministry. Rather, the apostle Paul's word to the Corinthians must serve as the North Star of our perspective, lighting up our skies as we sail through the uncharted waters of urban mission.

To change this metaphor for a moment, Paul challenged the Corinthians in 1 Corinthians 3.5-11 with a word concerning the importance of getting and keep the first things first:

> What then is Apollos? What is Paul? Servants through whom you believed, as the Lord assigned to each. I planted, Apollos watered, but God gave the growth. So neither he who plants nor he who waters is anything, but only God who gives the growth. He who plants and he who waters are one, and each will receive his wages according to his labor. For we are God's fellow workers. You are God's field, God's building. According to the grace of God given to me, like a skilled master builder I laid a foundation, and someone else is building upon it. Let each one take care how he builds upon it. For no one can lay a foundation other than that which is laid, which is Jesus Christ.

THE BOTTOM LINE FIRST:
JESUS CHRIST IS LORD OF ALL

Have this mind among yourselves, which is yours in Christ Jesus, who, though he was in the form of God, did not count equality with God a thing to be grasped, but emptied himself, by taking the form of a servant, being born in the likeness of men. And being found in human form, he humbled himself by becoming obedient to the point of death, even death on a cross. Therefore God has highly exalted him and bestowed on him the name that is above every name, so that at the name of Jesus every knee should bow, in heaven and on earth and under the earth, and every tongue confess that Jesus Christ is Lord, to the glory of God the Father.

~ Philippians 2.5-11

The most important truth in all the world is that Jesus of Nazareth is the Lord of all, head of the Church, and King of glory. He is God's chosen and anointed Messiah, the One whom God has selected to redeem the universe and restore humanity under his reign.

He has granted authority to his people to serve as his agents in the earth. At the center of the city throbs the question: "Who deserves to rule in this neighborhood/community/precinct/prison yard/city?"

YOU ARE NOT WHAT YOU APPEAR:
URBAN DISCIPLES ARE THE KEY TO THE CITY'S HEALING

See what kind of love the Father has given to us, that we should be called children of God; and so we are. The reason why the world does not know us is that it did not know him. Beloved, we are God's children now, and what we will be has not yet appeared; but we know that when he appears we shall be like him, because we shall see him as he is. And everyone who thus hopes in him purifies himself as he is pure.

~ 1 John 3.1-3

Urban Christians have been summarily overlooked and dismissed as key players in the great struggle for souls occurring in the cities of the world.

Actually, though, the answer to the transformation of America's cities is nothing less than the mobilization, equipping, and releasing of city Christians to penetrate their relationship networks with the Gospel of Christ.

As unlikely as it may appear, urban disciples are subject to the same stereotypes and low opinion as Nazareth was in Jesus' own day. (Recall Nathaniel's reply to Phillip after being told that Jesus, the Son of Joseph, from Nazareth, was in fact the Messiah, the very one whom Moses and the prophets wrote about.)

UNMOBILIZED MEANS UNUSED:
HOW THE DISUNITY OF URBAN BELIEVERS PROVIDES A FOOTHOLD FOR THE DEVIL IN THE CITY

> I therefore, a prisoner for the Lord, urge you to walk in a manner worthy of the calling to which you have been called, with all humility and gentleness, with patience, bearing with one another in love, eager to maintain the unity of the Spirit in the bond of peace. There is one body and one Spirit – just as you were called to the one hope that belongs to your call – one Lord, one faith, one baptism, one God and Father of all, who is over all and through all and in all. But grace was given to each one of us according to the measure of Christ's gift.
>
> ~ Ephesians 4.1-7

Nothing can dispute the radical and amazing power of unity. When any enterprise, team, or group unites around a common purpose and commitment, they are able to attain dramatic results, in both the natural and spiritual realms.

Today, urban churches are under siege – they often lack connection with other churches, struggle with countless moral issues, wrestle with all kinds of practical problems, and, on top of all these, also face the tricks of the devil, the temptations of the world, and the intimidating tactics of evil. All of these antagonists they may fight, in their own minds, by themselves, each one, disconnected, alone, and vulnerable.

Even when the tiniest creatures combine their energies and efforts around a common, central bond and goal, anchored in both shared perspectives and resources, they are able to accomplish great things, far more than what any one of them could have accomplished in their own strength and by their own efforts.

The devil knows that if he can keep urban churches and leaders from joining forces to seek the glory of Christ and the well-being of their neighborhoods, he can continue to ravage them. But, in order to do this, he must keep them from uniting together, from recognizing their need for each other, and from combining forces to attain God's purposes in their respective communities.

GOD'S CHOSEN METHOD TO HEAL THE CITY:
REDISCOVERING THE CENTRALITY OF THE CHURCH

I hope to come to you soon, but I am writing these things to you so that, if I delay, you may know how one ought to behave in the household of God, which is the church of the living God, a pillar and buttress of the truth. Great indeed, we confess, is the mystery of godliness: He was manifested in the flesh, vindicated by the Spirit, seen by angels, proclaimed among the nations, believed on in the world, taken up in glory.

~ 1 Timothy 3.14-16

The Church is the buttress, guardian, and foundation of the truth, the family of God, the body of Christ, and the temple of the Holy Spirit. She is God's mighty army, and granted spiritual weapons in order to engage the enemy and declare Jesus' victory to the nations.

Each local assembly of believers is a platoon, a righteous company of salvation called to represent Christ with honor in their locale, bearing witness to the Lord's kingdom victory to all in their sphere of influence.

This is why the SIAFU Network takes seriously the need for churches to approve and endorse this movement. We are unequivocal in stating that God's chosen means of transformation, his army, his deputy, is the Church. No lasting change will occur unless we as believers recognize our responsibility to stand up and represent Christ and his Kingdom with a new power and clarity. Without the Spirit reviving God's people, liberating them to do revolutionary, heroic acts of kingdom display and proclamation in the most dangerous communities on earth – without the Church being the Church, the city is lost.

But, thank God, Christ has stated clearly that no power of the dark side, of the gates of hell, can prevail against the holy aggression of the Church. Our weaponry is effective and devastating to the works of darkness – we need only move forward, under the Spirit's leading and empowerment. His words are as true today as they were when he spoke them to the apostles nearly two thousand years ago.

> Simon Peter replied, "You are the Christ, the Son of the living God." And Jesus answered him, "Blessed are you, Simon Bar-Jonah! For flesh and blood has not revealed this to you, but my Father who is in heaven. And I tell you, you are Peter, and on this rock I will build my church, and the gates of hell shall not prevail against it. I will give you the keys of the kingdom of heaven, and whatever you bind on earth shall be bound in heaven, and whatever you loose on earth shall be loosed in heaven."
>
> ~ Matthew 16.16-19

Christ is building his Church, and hell cannot defeat it! It is neither an exaggeration nor a falsehood to declare that "As the church goes, so the fight will go." When the Church (both global and local) awakens to its true identity as God's very own community, she will be released to become all she is in order that the kingdom light might be shown in the darkest and most dangerous places on earth.

REPORTING FOR DUTY:
WHY THE REDISCOVERY OF PASTORAL AUTHORITY REALLY MATTERS TO THE CITY

So I exhort the elders among you, as a fellow elder and a witness of the sufferings of Christ, as well as a partaker in the glory that is going to be revealed: shepherd the flock of God that is among you, exercising oversight, not under compulsion, but willingly, as God would have you; not for shameful gain, but eagerly; not domineering over those in your charge, but being examples to the flock. And when the chief Shepherd appears, you will receive the unfading crown of glory.

~ 1 Peter 5.1-4

Our God is the Sovereign God of the Universe, the God of Israel, and the God and Father of our Lord Jesus Christ. He is the Most High God, the one true Creator and Lord over all. No other gods or lords exist; he is solitary, supreme, and self-sufficient. Though his Son, our Lord Jesus, has been exalted to God's right hand (Phil. 2.5-11), his authority has not been recognized. At the heart of the city's greatest problem is the denial and rejection of legitimate spiritual authority. Rebellion and fragmentation are intrinsic to the city; many thousands of neighborhoods are suffering because urbanites have no spiritual head, nor do they submit to God's authority in his Church. If the local church is literally a platoon of the risen Christ, armed with the very powers of the Age to come for the sake of good, then there is no more important place in any city than a healthy, vital local church.

And, if this be the case, the most important office in the world is that of undershepherd of the Church, the pastor, i.e., those leaders entrusted with the watch care and oversight of the affairs of God's house. The Kingdom, first and foremost, is an exercise of the authority of the Lord Jesus, who himself in the Holy Spirit is subject to the authority of the Father.

No mobilization of the Church can occur without the clear, recognized blessing and support of its leaders. As God's servants to the body of Christ, they are the officers of the Lord under him, the Commander-in-Chief of God's Kingdom, and, as such, must give their blessing to any legitimate spiritual activity or initiative, in order for it to have God's blessing and provision.

If the cities of America are to have any chance of being redeemed and healed from the devil's tyranny, urban pastors must be released to be the kind of leaders worthy of the risen Christ, and be willing to lead their people in new, fresh ways in order that they may make a difference in the places now ravaged by the devil. The pastors, their hearts and minds, are the key to this transformation.

FOR CHAPTERS ON THE INSIDE

Your church- or ministry-sponsored SIAFU Chapter will be under the authority of the corrections facility. Although you should be free to minister to and encourage the men or women in your SIAFU Chapter, you have no spiritual authority over them. Continue to encourage, rebuke, exhort, challenge, build up, comfort and teach them but realize that all of their authority is in the corrections system they are a part of.

WE ALL "GOT THE GIFT":
THE UNIVERSAL PRIESTHOOD
OF THE BELIEVERS, URBAN STYLE

But you are a chosen race, a royal priesthood, a holy nation, a people for his own possession, that you may proclaim the excellencies of him who called you out of darkness into his marvelous light. Once you were not a people, but now you are God's people; once you had not received mercy, but now you have received mercy.

~ 1 Peter 2.9-10

For anyone to be a Christian, it means that they have possession of the Holy Spirit, who through the grace of Christ has endowed each believer with spiritual gifts for the sake of ministering to one another, and to those who do not know the Lord.

The communities of Christ were in fact "charismatic" assemblies, congregations where every believer, male or female, possessed divine endowments to be used for the good of all (see 1 Corinthains 12). These endowments were not earned, were not gender specific, and not mere talents or the result of natural abilities. They were divinely offered, potent and impacting, and often connected with divine manifestation and blessing (e.g., miracles in Galatians 3.5, spiritual prophesy in 1 Thessalonians 5.19-21, and a variety of manifestations in 1 Corinthians 12-14).

There can be no doubt; to be a disciple of Christ is to be a member of a priesthood whose origin is from God, one in which all who believe are granted gifts as God the Spirit has provided. Regardless of gender, class, culture, or race, if one confesses Jesus as Lord and believes that the Father has raised him from the dead, they receive eternal life. And, they are granted the indwelling and infilling of the Holy Spirit, along with the gifts and graces of the Lord.

This means every urban disciple has been granted the Holy Spirit and the endowments of the Lord in order to serve as Christ's ambassadors in the life situation and relational network where they live. This is the blessing and benefit of every believer, including city Christians, however poor and however small.

FREE TO LIVE, FREE TO LOVE:
URBAN DISCIPLES ARE LIBERATED IN CHRIST TO DO GOOD WORKS, WHENEVER WE CAN, WHEREVER WE ARE

> For you were called to freedom, brothers. Only do not use your freedom as an opportunity for the flesh, but through love serve one another. For the whole law is fulfilled in one word: "You shall love your neighbor as yourself." But if you bite and devour one another, watch out that you are not consumed by one another.
>
> ~ Galatians 5.13-15

Since all believers are given the Holy Spirit and the spiritual gifts of Christ to use for service and blessing, all have now been liberated in Christ to do good works. As a matter of fact, we were created in Christ Jesus as the very workmanship of God, in order that we might do good works, the very ones which we were reborn in Christ to accomplish (Eph. 2.8-10).

The potential for good works of love, hospitality, and generosity among urban Christians cannot possibly be calculated. Who knows the kind of healing and transformation that could occur in our urban neighborhoods if urban Christians, as priests of God and ambassadors for Christ, were to make themselves available to accomplish projects of servanthood in their communities, where they live and work?

The consistent apostolic exhortation to the young Christian communities in the New Testament was to do good works and so adorn (literally, "dress up") the high doctrine of God they had believed. Good works are accessible to anyone, regardless of how much money or influence they have. Anyone can serve, everyone can be kind, and participate in doing good. SIAFU will seek to inspire every urban Christian to be actively involved in a local assembly, and to make themselves available with others to do works worthy of the Father (Matt. 5.14-16).

CHOOSE A SIDE, MAKE A STAND:
WHY YOU AND YOUR CHURCH HAVE AN IMPORTANT PART TO PLAY IN YOUR CITY'S TRANSFORMATION

> So Ahab sent to all the people of Israel and gathered the prophets together at Mount Carmel. And Elijah came near to all the people and said, "How long will you go limping between two different opinions? If the Lord is God, follow him; but if Baal, then follow him." And the people did not answer him a word.
>
> ~ 1 Kings 18.20-21

In a fight as cosmic as the spiritual battle of the ages, and in a battle as important as the very survival of our cities, no urban church, or urban leader, or urban Christian can afford to sit on the sidelines, avoiding the conflict that ultimately will touch us all.

You and your church must declare yourselves on the Lord's side. Like young David, you must stir yourselves up against any and all opposition to the Kingdom of God, and make yourselves available to do whatever you can to represent the Nazarene with honor where you are.

Let urban disciples of Jesus respond to his call, making themselves available to be used of the Lord to do whatever is necessary to see the Kingdom of God advanced, the Gospel declared, and the wholeness, freedom, and justice of God's reign displayed in their good works in their neighborhoods, for Christ's glory. No one can afford to neglect this call. Let all who can, enlist in this great army, allowing themselves to be equipped, so the great Captain of their salvation may deploy them wherever he will.

NOT BY POWER, NOR BY MIGHT:
REVIVAL THROUGH THE POWER OF THE HOLY SPIRIT CAN TRANSFORM THE NEIGHBORHOOD

Then he said to me, "This is the word of the Lord to Zerubbabel:
Not by might, nor by power, but by my Spirit, says the Lord of hosts.

~ Zechariah 4.6

Sincerity, however, will not be enough. All of the good intentions and high and most sincere promises and vows to God will fall short without his divine intervention and visitation.

The power of God, specifically, the power of the Holy Spirit, is the provision the Father has granted us in order that we might represent the Kingdom with honor and clarity. Without the Holy Spirit, all our efforts and activities will prove to be futile and useless against the tactics and deception of the enemy.

If the apostles of Jesus had to remain in Jerusalem, waiting to declare the Gospel until the power of the Holy Spirit fell on them, how much more will urban Christians need to gather and wait on God to endue them with power from on high, before they can win their families, their neighborhoods, and cities for Christ!

TO THE ENDS OF THE EARTH:
WE MUST MOBILIZE EVERY AVAILABLE URBAN CHRISTIAN TO JOIN THE MOVEMENT TO FULFILL THE GREAT COMMISSION IN OUR LIFETIME

> And Jesus came and said to them, "All authority in heaven and on earth has been given to me. Go therefore and make disciples of all nations, baptizing them in the name of the Father and of the Son and of the Holy Spirit, teaching them to observe all that I have commanded you. And behold, I am with you always, to the end of the age."
>
> ~ Matthew 28.18-20

Every boy, girl, woman, and man in the city deserves a chance to hear the Good News of God's salvation offer in Jesus Christ. The Church is called to make disciples of Christ, baptizing them in the name of the triune God, and teaching each convert all that Christ has commanded us (Matt. 28.18-19). This Commission is given to the urban church as well.

We must find efficient, credible, and effective ways to recruit urban Christians to the fight, to equip them for battle against the devil and his agents, and then, in Christ's name and for his glory, to see them released to touch their friends, families, associates, and neighbors with the love of God.

If the urban neighborhoods around the world are to be won, they must be won by urban disciples of Christ, men and women, boys and girls, who have been touched by the fire of God, who have been trained in the Word of God, and who, in unity and love, band together with others to do good works for the Lord where they live, and work, and play.

SIAFU represents a practical, efficient way to gather urban Christians together, to inspire them with the message of Christ, to equip them for the work of the ministry, and then to challenge them to serve and share in their own networks for the sake of Christ.

PART II:
MAKING THE CASE
WHY YOU NEED A SIAFU CHAPTER IN YOUR CHURCH

SETTING FORTH OUR CASE:
ANSWERING THE OBJECTIONS TO MOBILIZING URBAN DISCIPLES FOR REVIVAL IN THE CITIES OF AMERICA

The promise of a revived urban America is desirable, but that does not mean that the SIAFU Network or any other national initiative has God's blessing or should be supported. In order to deal bluntly and clearly with the major objections to starting a SIAFU Chapter, we have listed ten clear, credible objections to the whole idea of SIAFU. Other movements have come and gone and have given the same sales pitch. They tend to entice urban churches and urban leaders to "get on the bandwagon," and essentially join them. SIAFU's entire orientation, however, is completely different.

The basic assumption of the SIAFU Network is that if God is going to reach and transform the ailing inner cities of America, he will do this through healthy, vital church movements which spring up in neighborhoods, and then do the work of the Kingdom in the midst of their neighbors. City folk will be God's means to reach city folk. If this thesis is true, then any movement that tends to want to support city folk must answer the objections directly, honestly, and forthrightly.

This entire part of the guidebook is designed to highlight a critical objection, give an answer concisely and clearly, and then provide a little commentary that discusses both the objection and the answer. Of course, we are neither suggesting nor contending that only ten objections exist concerning SIAFU. (Perhaps you will think of other questions and objections, which we will be happy to address directly through our contact section on our SIAFU website page). The point in this exercise is not only to answer these objections, but also to demonstrate our openness in the Network to deal with thorny, hard issues with an open heart and mind. If the SIAFU Network is from the Lord, it will pursue the truth in all things, as the truth will certainly set us free to accomplish the will of God together, as the Spirit leads (John 8.31-32).

The objections are not listed in any ascending or descending order, or given in some rising sense of difficulty or priority. We have sought to think of the most obvious and difficult questions that might arise as you ponder the possibility of starting your own SIAFU Chapter, and did our best to provide immediate and clear feedback on them. Use the objections below to clarify your own thinking. Our prayer is that the discussions will help you better understand what SIAFU is, and what its potential is for helping you take your city for the Lord.

THE ORIGIN OF THE SIAFU MOVEMENT: THE MINISTRY OF WORLD IMPACT

The SIAFU movement grew out of the efforts of World Impact to fully engage and rely upon the leaders, workers, and Christian ministers that God was raising up in places long overlooked and ignored, places such as poor urban neighborhoods, prison yards, and rescue missions. World Impact is a Christian mission's organization committed to facilitating church planting movements by evangelizing, equipping, and empowering America's urban poor. Its vision is to recruit, empower, and release urban leaders who will plant churches and launch indigenous church planting movements.

This entire movement of healthy gatherings of zealous disciples of Jesus was born out of our confidence in what almighty God can do through the lives of those who for generations have been oppressed, discarded, forgotten, and underestimated – those in prison, the broken and despised, those whom others have given up on. Truly, however, our God has chosen these folk to be his very champions, the very ones he intends to use to bring himself glory.

> "For consider your calling, brethren, that there were not many wise according to the flesh, not many mighty, not many noble; [27] but God has chosen the foolish things of the world to shame the wise, and God has chosen the weak things of the world to shame the things which are strong, [28] and the base things of the world and the despised God has chosen, the things that are not, so that He may nullify the things that are, [29] so that no man may boast before God."
>
> ~ 1 Corinthians 1.26-29

Our entire understanding can be summed up in this way: we believe that God can use anyone he selects, regardless of the circumstances or conditions they have come from, to impact others for good, right where they live. This includes especially their own unique network of personal relationships – family, friends, associates, others imprisoned with them. God raises up men and women, boys and girls to impact their worlds, i.e., their *oikos* (network of influence), those who know them, have known them, or are related in some way to them.

God chooses and promotes what most folk discard and throw away. He makes people new, and uses them in mighty ways. This is the heart of the SIAFU movement and the joyful confession of every SIAFU Chapter.

OBJECTION 1:
WE ALREADY HAVE A FINE YOUNG ADULT AND ADULT MINISTRY, AND THEREFORE HAVE NO NEED FOR A SIAFU CHAPTER.

The Argument: "Our pastor doesn't believe we need one. He believes that the Lord has blessed our Women's and Men's Ministry, and feels we already have a group to meet the needs of those in our congregation. We don't need no Chapters in our church!"

The Answer: Praise God for your adult ministry efforts! SIAFU may not be right for you, or it may actually strengthen your current work even more.

We wholeheartedly support and affirm the pastor's and/or leadership team's assessment of your adult ministry group. Continue to increase and abound in your great efforts, seeking the Holy Spirit's direction in your work.

SIAFU, however, ought not necessarily be seen as a replacement for your own fine ministry, but as an opportunity to both extend and enhance it. It extends the borders of your group, connecting it with others in your locale, state, region, and across the country. It enhances your group by integrating you with dozens of other churches who also host Chapters, giving you a platform for relationship, contact, and cooperation with others who share your vision and commitment to men and women, and to the transformation of the city in Christ's name.

The SIAFU Network is neither a competition nor an antagonism. We celebrate every strong association that is occurring between and among urban churches and urban Christian leaders, and pray that SIAFU will add to the number and quality of strong partnerships among Christian churches everywhere!

OBJECTION 2:

THE PUNY ACTIONS OF A SINGLE, LITTLE URBAN CHURCH CAN'T POSSIBLY MAKE A DIFFERENCE ON THE MASSIVE PROBLEMS OF OUR CITY.

The Argument: "Our city is so big and intimidating and sick. We're such a small congregation with very limited resources – we don't have much money, we have very few folk who are faithful, and we are lucky if we get them interested in our own activities, let alone some outside group. Maybe if we were bigger, a little stronger, we might consider it. We're barely surviving now – how can we do something like this?"

The Answer: SIAFU is designed to connect your church's efforts and activities to those of thousands of others Chapters nationwide.

Your sense of the intimidation of the city and the smallness of your footprint within it is well defined. We can easily become overwhelmed when we view the hulkiness and unholiness of urban sprawl on our own, through the lens of our little local "platoon," viewing the city's wildness and oppression without the support, encouragement, and challenge of other churches and leaders.

The SIAFU Network is specifically designed to fight against the tendency to see the entire fight against the enemy in the cities where we live through the resources of our own small congregation. This is akin to the ten spies who, after looking at the cities of Canaan with their fortifications and armaments, felt that entering the Promised Land was futile and wrong. Viewing the forces of evil over against your own meager personal resources can easily intimidate and confuse.

In a similar way, if we view the city only through the lens of our own church's resources and activities, it is very easy to become overpowered, confused, and disturbed. You should consider starting a Chapter to connect your efforts to those of thousands of others who share your love for Christ and for the city.

OBJECTION 3:
We are skeptical about the motives of SIAFU; shouldn't we be more than a little suspicious of any outside influences on our church?

The Argument: "We are doubtful about SIAFU and what its motives might be. Why should we set up another structure in our church, Chapters or anything else? You can never be too careful when some outside organization wants to tinker around in our life together. How do we know that folk won't use this as a pretense to mess with our church?"

The Answer: SIAFU only operates under the blessing and authority of the leaders in the congregations that host its Chapters.

The SIAFU Network was designed intentionally to operate only with the full blessing of the leaders of the congregation. In other words, unless the pastor or leaders of the congregation or organization grant their explicit permission for a Chapter to function in the church, no Chapter will operate. Furthermore, Chapters cannot function on their own; they must convince the pastor and/or leaders of the church or organization that a Chapter would edify and strengthen their life together, or they will never be approved to start.

Since we believe that the Church is the pillar and ground of the truth (and not a SIAFU Chapter!), we affirm that our allegiance to the Lord Jesus Christ is demonstrated through our connection and submission to legitimate pastoral authority in a church. SIAFU Chapters do not stand alone; they require a church or Christian organization's endorsement and permission to operate.

We blocked out the SIAFU Network to always function in response to and under the authority of the pastor or leaders of the congregation or organization to avoid any appearance of outside interference in the life of the church. No Chapter can be in commission without the knowledge and blessing of the spiritual leaders where the Chapter is hosted.

OBJECTION 4:
CHAPTERS MAY COME TO ACTUALLY INTERFERE WITH OUR CHURCH'S DIRECTION AND LEADERSHIP.

The Argument: "Setting up a SIAFU Chapter in our church may easily lead to conflict among our leaders. How do we give oversight to the Chapter and make it conform to our understanding of church government and leadership? Whenever you have new groups you run the risk of sowing seeds of division and conflict of interest. It's hard to trust folk you don't know. How can we protect ourselves from weird leaders who come in and try to take over things relevant to our church?"

The Answer: The goal of a SIAFU Chapter is to cultivate spiritual formation under the oversight of the church's/organization's leadership.

It is important to note that no SIAFU Chapter is legitimate that refuses to acknowledge and obey the oversight of the leaders in the church. The SIAFU Network recognizes and boldly affirms the local assembly as the locus and agent of the Kingdom of God in a given locale.

SIAFU is not meant to be viewed as a substitute church, nor an alternative to membership in a Christian local assembly. No SIAFU Chapter is legitimate if the pastors and/or leaders forbid its gathering in their church or organization. You will only run the risk of division if you shortchange the importance of the local church, of membership and connection to the local assembly, and submission to pastoral authority. No one and no organization should intrude in the governance of a local assembly; the Holy Spirit, acting and moving those leaders he has made overseers, is how the church must be run, for Jesus' sake.

The end game of SIAFU Chapter activity is evangelizing and equipping men and women to be disciples of Christ, fleshing that discipleship out in the context of the local assembly under pastoral authority. It must never be to interfere with the workings and direction of the Lord through the church. This is the way it was conceived, and how it should operate, in every case.

The following saying stands in regard to all things related to the SIAFU Network: "No church, no SIAFU. Know church, know SIAFU!"

FOR CHAPTERS ON THE INSIDE

Your church- or ministry-sponsored SIAFU Chapter will be under the authority of the corrections facility. Although you should be free to minister to and encourage the men or women in your SIAFU Chapter, you have no spiritual authority over them. Continue to encourage, rebuke, exhort, challenge, build up, comfort and teach them but realize that all of their authority is in the corrections system they are a part of.

OBJECTION 5:
WE DON'T HAVE A WAY TO INTEGRATE FOLK WHO ARE "DIFFERENT" INTO OUR CHURCH.

The Argument: "I like the idea of a SIAFU Chapter in our church, but I am genuinely afraid that if the Lord were to bring us really different kinds of folk, our church wouldn't accept them. We're not prepared to welcome ex-prisoners, ex-gang bangers and folk like that into our church. It sounds good, but I don't know how they would fit. Beside, it would make a lot of our members feel uncomfortable having folk like that around."

The Answer: We should expect the Word of God to convert and call men and women from the city to the Lord, and SIAFU Chapters are an effective means to incorporate new and immature Christians into our churches.

In many urban churches, we oftentimes do not have a safe, open, and welcoming place for church members to invite their lost neighbors, friends, and family to hear the Gospel. To be sure, we can always invite them to our special outreaches, our worship services, and evangelistic meetings, but these can be intimidating to lost people, especially when they realize they are being "targeted" in such meetings.

SIAFU Chapters can allow you to host small, non-intimidating, and culturally sensitive gatherings where people can be introduced to the Lord through the testimony and experience of ordinary believers. In the same way that groups like Alcoholics Anonymous have been able to create a warm, safe place for people to come and be exposed to sobriety, so SIAFU Chapters will provide the same warm environment for church members to invite seekers to attend, and be exposed to men and women who love and serve the Lord.

Of course, we know that the goal of the Gospel is to bring every person into the Kingdom of God, for it is the power of God for salvation to each one who believes (Rom. 1.16). This includes those described as unlovely, unlikely, and even "dangerous." The goal of all Christian ministry is to bring folk into the body of Christ, to incorporate them into Christ's church as full members and recipients of the grace of God.

Moreover, SIAFU Chapters can allow you a means by which you can incorporate new and immature urban Christians into your church. It allows you to gather where they can hear the Good News, and befriend and incorporate those who repent and believe. It allows you encourage them in their faith and challenge them to be disciples. Since every Chapter sponsors service projects for the benefit of the church and community, it will also allow them to learn how to do good works, how to engage in practical efforts of care and servanthood, and how to be hospitable and generous.

In other words, simply saying that your church is inhospitable to sinners is no excuse for disobeying our Lord in receiving those who repent and believe into our family! Remember, the Gospel is the power of God for salvation to everyone who believes – every person who is saved is also an ex-offender (including you)!

OBJECTION 6:
WE DON'T HAVE ANYONE TO GIVE OVERSIGHT TO A SIAFU CHAPTER.

The Argument: "Frankly, the idea of a SIAFU Chapter sounds great, but we currently don't have men or women who could lead such a Chapter. We're a small church with very few faithful leaders, and right now they are currently tied up with the other business of the church. We can't afford to spread them too thin on a new, risky outreach kind of thing like SIAFU right now. Maybe we'll consider it when we have more leaders available to lead it."

The Answer: SIAFU Chapters function as incubators, literally, greenhouses, for servant leadership development.

One of the greatest benefits of a SIAFU Chapter is its ability to provide urban churches with a built-in structure where emerging leaders can come and learn to lead. The Chapter is set up in such a way that growing Christian leaders can come, under pastoral authority, and learn how to host a meeting, to pray for others, and to prove themselves capable, sacrificial servant leaders, for the well-being of the church.

In this sense, SIAFU Chapters operate as an incubator, as a greenhouse of growing and cultivating solid Christian servant leaders. As such, it can solve the problem of local urban churches which have few or no urban leaders by creating the condition where we produce new ones, a class of servant leaders who open themselves up to healing their neighborhoods instead of avoiding them.

Servanthood is a call that any urban person can fulfill, regardless of their education level, social class, or current skill set. Anyone can learn to serve, to care, to help others. SIAFU Chapters will encourage all to give what they have, to be faithful, available, teachable, and open. Every person in the church is given gifts of the Spirit and can be trained to be a servant.

OBJECTION 7:
WE ALREADY HAVE A NETWORK OF OTHER CHURCHES WE RELATE TO, AND ENJOY GREAT FELLOWSHIP AND COLLABORATION TOGETHER.

The Argument: "Although the SIAFU Network sounds great, we already are a part of a healthy association and denomination which serves our needs wonderfully. We meet together regularly, do outreaches together, and fellowship in one another's churches often. I really don't see the need for joining this network when our current associations are so healthy and are working so well for us."

The Answer: The SIAFU Network affirms all healthy church and Christian associations and seeks to both enrich and broaden their impact and effect.

SIAFU Chapters unashamedly affirm the necessity of Christian unity and renewal, especially among individual congregations and urban connections. The Network was conceived with the burden of finding ways to encourage the priority of urban disciples and urban congregations working together, respecting and befriending one another for the sake of the Kingdom. If your church is a part of a vital network, by no means should you exit or tamper with it! This is precisely what the SIAFU Network is seeking to inspire and instigate.

Still, the SIAFU Network may enrich your current association, given its scope and broad clientele. We believe that urban Christians are part of a larger connection, related to their unique experience as urban dwellers in at-risk communities. They all share the same longings, difficulties, experiences, vulnerabilities, and challenges. Because of their shared experience with those not only in their locale but across the country, they can be welcomed into a larger network which can only build up their association.

Since SIAFU is a national network of urban churches and leaders, you should consider joining the Network for greater exposure of your own association, for making new friends who share your burdens and goals, in different places across the country. Without question, the real possibility exists that, when you join the Network, you will be able to expose other Chapters to what you are doing on the battlefield of Christ where you live and work. Such exposure will allow them to plagiarize your good practices!

Surely then, you can see how strategic SIAFU can be for your church, especially so if it is healthy, vital, and growing.

OBJECTION 8:
SIAFU WAS STARTED BY AN OUTSIDE GROUP, WHOSE MEMBERS AND CULTURE ARE DEFINITELY NOT FROM THE HOOD!

The Argument: "While the prospect of SIAFU is a great idea, the problem with it is that it was started by a group made up of virtually no city people, most of whom have never lived in the hood or even can begin to understand what life is like in it. SIAFU would have been a fine thing if it had been started by urban folk, but, as it is, World Impact is mainly a white, suburban, and outside-the-hood kind of organization.

The Answer: The SIAFU Network was created because we believe that only urban churches and disciples of Christ will win the cities of America and the world.

Since our founding more than forty years ago, World Impact (TUMI's parent organization) has spoken prophetically regarding God's election of the poor, the benign neglect of the evangelical church of America's inner-city poor, and the need for evangelism, discipleship, and church planting in unreached urban poor communities. We believe that credible urban mission must demonstrate the Gospel, testifying in both the proclaimed word and concrete action.

In light of this, we have emphasized living in the communities we serve, ministering to the needs of the whole person, as well as to the members of the whole urban family. We have sought this witness with a goal to see communities reached and transformed by Christ, believing that those who live in the city and are poor can be empowered to live in the freedom, wholeness, and justice of the Kingdom of God fleshed out in local churches and viable urban church planting movements. All World Impact's vision, prayer, and efforts have concentrated on those most unfortunate, seeking to win them to Christ, equip them in the faith, and empower them through all facets of our work. From church planting to forming schools and clinics, to hosting camps, all we have done has been designed to empower urban Christians to win those in their own neighborhoods.

Everything World Impact has initiated, including our TUMI ministry, has been for the purpose of empowering urban churches and their leaders to reach and transform their own communities for Christ – in the Holy Spirit, only urban folk can be empowered to win and equip urban folk!

Outside organizations like World Impact may empower urban churches to accomplish the Great Commission in the city, but ultimately these outside groups will never be the agents through which God transforms the city. This is why we started SIAFU, to assist urban churches to form a network where urban believers can befriend, equip, and challenge one another to fulfill Christ's commission in the city (Matt. 28.18-20).

In the final analysis, only urban disciples will prove effective in making urban disciples. The SIAFU Network is anchored on this key biblical insight.

FOR CHAPTERS ON THE INSIDE

A SIAFU Chapter requires stable, on-going leadership to be fruitful over time. Since population terms are both volatile and unknown in most prison settings, with much turnover occurring at a rapid rate (e.g., among inmates, chaplains, prison officials, and volunteers), SIAFU programs with leadership by a church on the outside are likely to be far more stable and effective.

In addition, a church on the outside that sponsors a SIAFU Chapter can use its chapter program to do outreach inside the walls. It can also more naturally provide a pathway to incorporate returning citizens to its fellowship, once members are released on the outside. In other words, when an effective SIAFU identity is established on the inside, it will be more natural to connect with a SIAFU Chapter on the outside. The chances for real, lasting relationships are significantly increased when returning citizens upon release attend and participate in the sponsoring SIAFU-hosting church.

Another key benefit for outside sponsorship of SIAFU chapters are the links that can be made to TUMI satellites, especially in those churches which sponsor both programs on the outside.

OBJECTION 9:

SIAFU IS NO PANACEA FOR THE CITY; ON ITS OWN, WITHOUT GOD'S DIRECT BLESSING AND VISITATION, THE SIAFU NETWORK WILL NEVER ACCOMPLISH ITS HIGH GOALS.

The Argument: "You are talking as if SIAFU, in and of itself, is something special and that it will be the thing that makes the difference in the city. This is contrary to experience and to Scripture. The city is so messed up, so big, so intimidating that it would take a God to change it. A few scrawny little Chapters of ex-jacked-up folk will not change the city. We need to depend on God to do that, because he is the only one who can get that done!"

The Answer: SIAFU engages its members at the local level, but it is an association of Chapters connected all across the nation. It is a local as well as a regional and national entity.

We initiated the SIAFU Network out of a profound sense of neediness, fueled by an inner awareness that all of the work that we seek to accomplish for the Lord in the city would be utterly futile if the Lord failed "to show up and show out" in the mean streets of American ghettos. The crime, the broken homes, the economic blight, and the spiritual darkness continue to settle over thousands of communities, none of which has ever seen or heard of the triumphant victory our Lord Jesus Christ won for them in his incarnation, death, resurrection, and ascension. They are lost and without God in the world.

Add to these troubling facts, the additional realization that millions of people continue to languish under the gray skies of the devil's lies and tyranny, existing without hope and with no knowledge of Christ at all. In neighborhoods ravaged by violence and poverty, they struggle to find meaning, and live on the cruel borders of self-loathing and despair.

These truths lead to one clear conclusion. With untold thousands of communities under the sway of the enemy, we are convinced that only the Lord can change the city. Neither SIAFU, nor TUMI, nor World

Impact, nor any other Christian organization or program can possibly pierce through the darkness that enshrouds our cities, here in America and around the world. Only the living Christ can transform the cities; only a visitation from the Lord will make the difference.

We completely agree with the view that SIAFU cannot be seen as a "magic bullet" of ministry for urban America. What it can do, however, is connect urban churches, urban leaders, and urban disciples under a common purpose and vision to see Christ glorified in their neighborhoods. Knowing that you are one of perhaps hundreds of Chapters of other urban disciples who are seeking God's power to transform their cities can inspire, challenge, and bless you to keep fighting.

In addition, connecting with urban Christians from around the country can provide you with the stimulation and vision to start new initiatives and projects designed to make a difference in your church and neighborhood. And, collaborating with other Chapters in your locale can spark new partnerships and sponsorships for sharing the Good News in practical, amazing ways.

SIAFU, then, is not a panacea, or a magic bullet. However, it can be a legitimate, traction-building tool that urban churches can use to further their goals of spiritual formation and mission in the city. These Chapters, under the authority of local leadership and vision, can become an effective means by which we can befriend, encourage, and challenge urban churches and disciples to honor God, right where we live, here and now.

OBJECTION 10:
WE WANT TO START A SIAFU CHAPTER, BUT WE DON'T KNOW HOW.

The Argument: "Okay, we're convinced we should start a Chapter, but we do not have a clue how to start one. How does it work? Does it cost any money? Who is in charge of it, and are there any dues to pay? What if we want to end our Chapter – what then? We have so many questions, and don't know how to get answers to them!"

The Answer: TUMI administrates the SIAFU Network in order to provide urban churches with the administrative and resource support to host effective, vital Chapters in their locales.

As an organization whose purpose is to equip leaders for the urban church, TUMI is dedicated to facilitating movements like the SIAFU Network for urban mission. We established the Network because of our deep faith in the power of urban spirituality. When urban churches and their leaders are empowered by the Holy Spirit for ministry and mission, fruit is borne, for God's glory!

In the same way that we resource our training satellites here in America and around the world, so we are also committed to doing whatever we can to strengthen those in the SIAFU Network, in order that they can fulfill God's purposes in the city. As God has chosen the poor to be rich in faith and heirs to the Kingdom of God (James 2.5), we count it a high honor to support the Network with solid, efficient, and clear processes for starting and running your Chapter.

SIAFU is meant to be a resource for urban churches, one which they find useful and handy, and one which eliminates headaches and questions for them! We have sought to make the initiation steps simple and clear, to create resources that are both affordable and helpful, and to keep all policies and processes connected with it culturally sensitive and responsive to local church authority. We desire the SIAFU Network to be a blessing, not a burden, financially or administratively.

Specifically, we wrote this guidebook in order to provide you with a one-stop shop to know how to form, launch, and operate a SIAFU Chapter in your church or organization. We will provide ongoing online support at our website, along with additional resources designed to help you host your Chapter and watch it grow as the Lord uses it within your church and community.

The answers to these objections make plain the need we have to start and host SIAFU Chapters in urban churches all across America. God's chosen method of transformation and proclamation is the Church, which is the place where God's Spirit dwells and whose work advances the Kingdom of God. SIAFU Chapters do not stand alone; they require the blessing and endorsement of pastoral/leadership authority.

The SIAFU Network empowers local urban churches to identify, equip and release servant leaders who can make a difference where they live. It is a network that helps urban churches mobilize their members to follow Christ and be fruitful for the gospel. Our intent is to challenge the whole next generation of urban Christians to minister to urban Christians, to befriend, equip, and disciple urbanites, who will join urban churches which can continue to advance the Kingdom.

We chose the motif of the SIAFU ants because of their shared commitment to their common welfare. As vulnerable as these little creatures are as individuals, they are formidable and powerful when they stand together. They accomplish remarkable things when they work together for a common aim. As a colony of millions of individuals per nest, the SIAFU are truly a force to be reckoned with, one that is not easily impeded or stopped. In the same way, urban churches and disciples can be a force for the Kingdom of God if they make it their common shared aim to represent the Kingdom of God in their cities.

Whether a SIAFU Chapter has only 3 people or 303 members, each Chapter will know that they are not alone but a part of a larger group of believers throughout their city and beyond. As a community committed to the local church, our hope is that urban disciples will band together to pray, share the Good News, serve and care for each other and their community. We are convinced that urbanites will be used of the Holy Spirit to win the lost, disciple the saved, plant new churches, start new ministries, and honor God in dramatic new ways in the city. These church Chapters can transform their communities and their families and represent Christ and his Kingdom in their neighborhoods and cities. God can make it happen.

If you believe this and want to participate by forming your own Chapter, keep reading. Part III explains how you can start a SIAFU Chapter in your own church or Christian organization and begin to create an environment where urban disciples can be befriended, equipped, and released for ministry!

PART III:
FORMING A COMPANY
THE HOW-TO'S OF STARTING YOUR SIAFU CHAPTER

ORGANIZING FOR CHANGE:
STARTING YOUR OWN CHAPTER OF THE SIAFU NETWORK

FIRST THINGS FIRST

Now that we have laid out the reasons why we need to mobilize urban disciples to touch and transform their churches and neighborhoods, we are ready to talk about the specifics of starting your own Chapter. We have sought to make this as transparent and simple as possible; the desire is to create a process that churches all across the country can follow, linking the various Chapters together with a common vision and burden: to transform America's inner cities for Christ.

To begin with, you must take stock in your present relationship with Christ. You should start this process with the truth – clearly know your commitment to the Lord, his Church, his people, your city, and the neighborhood where your Chapter will meet. You will need to seek the Lord regarding the shape and status of your Chapter, spend ample time discussing the implications of the Chapter with your pastoral and spiritual authority, and move forward boldly and wisely, as God leads.

The following steps and structure are designed to help you become as clear as possible about your Chapter – what your Chapter will be, how and when you will start, how you will function, and why you started. Get together those interested in starting a SIAFU Chapter, and begin to brainstorm on some of the things you hope to accomplish through your group. Discuss together your vision for what you believe God wants to do through your Chapter. Questions like these may trigger some good ideas in your discussion:

- Why do we want a SIAFU Chapter? What do we hope God will accomplish through our group in the weeks and months ahead?

- When do we want to start our Chapter, and when will we sponsor our gatherings? How often will we meet, and where will the meetings be held?

- Who are the people we will want to attend, in the short run? In the long run, what other folk or groups do we hope to target with our Chapter?

- How will our particular Chapter relate to the pastor and/or ministry leader team?

- What kind of activities do we foresee our Chapter sponsoring right away?

HOW TO FORM YOUR SIAFU NETWORK CHAPTER:
A STEP-BY-STEP GUIDE

STEP ONE

Familiarize yourself with all materials and videos connected to the SIAFU Network. Read through the written materials you have seen and received, whether our brochures or write-ups on our SIAFU website. Watch the short videos on SIAFU to find out specific information about this church-based ministry opportunity. Also, make sure that you check our FAQ page (which stands for *Frequently Asked Questions*) to read questions and answers that have been asked about SIAFU. Use these materials and videos to discern God's will and timing for your SIAFU Chapter, when you should start and how you will pursue it in your church or organization.

* Introduction to SIAFU (visit www.tumi.org/siafu.intro)

* SIAFU and the Local Church (visit www.tumi.org/siafu.church)

* What is SIAFU, and why is it an important opportunity for your church? (www.tumi.org/siafu.video)

STEP TWO

Carefully think through the arguments of the SIAFU Network Guidebook, especially the points made and stressed in Parts I and II. Study this Guide-book, making sure you understand what the Network is, and how to begin the process to form your Chapter. (This *SIAFU Network Guidebook* is our official how-to guidebook for churches and organizations considering establishing their own Chapter in their church.)

We designed this resource specifically to guide you through the rationale and process of starting a Chapter in your church. We are absolutely convinced that the Church is the best venue for pastoral care, encouragement, and service. This workbook is informed by that conviction and will give you all you need to start your Chapter. Any questions you have about what a SIAFU Chapter is or how to form one in your church is here laid out in plain language. Make sure that you don't rush through it; take the time to "get the pulse" of what this movement is, and count the cost on what God is saying to you about it.

Step Three

Fill out the necessary application and reference forms and submit them to TUMI for processing. Complete the *SIAFU Chapter Online Application* and email the link of the *Pastor's Reference Form* to your pastor or ministry leader. You can find these online sources here:

- SIAFU Online Application (www.tumi.org/siafu.application)

- Online Pastor's Reference Form (www.tumi.org/siafu.reference)

Step Four

Wait for notification from TUMI regarding the status of your application. Once we receive your application and reference forms, we will promptly review your application materials and as soon as possible notify you by email of your acceptance as a SIAFU Chapter. Our intent is to treat each application as a priority event; we will do all in our power to contact you promptly after your submission of all the necessary materials.

Step Five

Receive notification of your acceptance, and take all necessary actions and efforts to set up your Chapter. Once we have contacted you regarding your acceptance status, then it will be time to begin to set up your Chapter. We have created a *Chapter Launch Checklist* which you should use to make certain that you follow all the necessary steps to start your Chapter. This is important, for all SIAFU Chapters will be set up according to a single SIAFU standard protocol. This Checklist will prove to be a handy guide for you as you think through the various pieces of your Chapter. Please note: the *Chapter Launch Checklist* was developed as a helpful guide for you, and does not need to be submitted to TUMI.

You can find the *Chapter Launch Checklist* in the Appendix of this Guidebook, as well as on our website at *www.tumi.org/siafu.checklist.*

STEP SIX

Fill out the online Chapter Completion Form for your approved SIAFU Chapter (and pay the one time, Chapter start-up fee).*

*The one-time, Chapter start-up fee is calculated on a sliding fee scale based on the approximate number of individuals your church or organization serves on a monthly basis. This is an honor system; whatever estimate you provide will be accepted, and you can then pay the fee associated with your guestimate. The scale is below:

- 1-50 individuals served monthly   .   .   . $50

- 51-100 individuals served monthly .   .   . $75

- 101-250 individuals served monthly   .   . $100

- 251 and up individuals served monthly .   . $150

Please note, there is an annual Chapter renewal fee of $25 along with your continued affirmation of our Statement of Faith (due January 31 after the first full year of membership).

The Checklist will help you think through the various elements you'll want to plan in starting your Chapter. Once you have thought through these important matters for your Chapter, you'll be ready to submit your *Chapter Completion Form* and pay the setup fee. You can find this form on the SIAFU website at the following url:

- Online Chapter Completion Form (*www.tumi.org/siafu.completion*)

STEP SEVEN

Finally, receive your user name and password to the SIAFU Network Chapter website. Once you have submitted the *Chapter Completion Form* and paid your fee, we will send you a user name and password for the SIAFU website (immediately emailed once we receive your form), and will sign you up for the SIAFU monthly newsletter. We will also send you your complimentary *SIAFU Chapter Resource Kit** which will provide you with helpful materials and tools to help get your Chapter up and running.

*The SIAFU Chapter Resource Kit contains the following:

- One official, embossed SIAFU Certificate printed with your Chapter Name (for approved SIAFU Chapters)

- One additional *SIAFU Network Guidebook*

- Two *SIAFU Network Chapter Meeting Guides*

- One *Let God Arise! Prayer Booklet* with a pack of ten brochures

- Twenty SIAFU Network brochures

- One copy of the *Mo' Power* Spiritual Warfare Series CD (which contains a digital studio mixed version of the *SIAFU Chant*)

- One 24" x 36" SIAFU poster

Congratulations! Once these steps have been completed you will become an official SIAFU Chapter. Count on us to do all we can to stand with you as you seek to encourage, equip, and resource the men and women in your church to represent Christ with each other, in your body, and in your community.

Please check our SIAFU online newsletters and website often for special offers and resources to enhance and strengthen your Chapter activities.

HOW TO RUN YOUR SIAFU NETWORK CHAPTER:
OFFICERS AND PROCEDURES

THE SIAFU CHAPTER:
THE BASIC BUILDING BLOCK OF THE SIAFU NETWORK

The basic element in the SIAFU Network is the SIAFU Chapter. SIAFU Chapters are related to one another as siblings, as brothers and sisters. In other words, every SIAFU Chapter runs and operates individually under its own vision and authority as permitted by its pastoral and/or spiritual authority. Each SIAFU Chapter, therefore, is autonomous and free to operate and function under the authority of its local pastor and/or spiritual director.

RELATIONSHIP OF SIAFU CHAPTERS TO
TUMI AND THE OTHER MEMBER CHAPTERS

Regionally or locally, SIAFU Chapters may decide to gather and collaborate for the sake of worship, fellowship, service, and mission in their locale or city. Currently *The Urban Ministry Institute*, a ministry of *World Impact, Inc.*, resources and coordinates the national communication on behalf of the SIAFU Network. TUMI processes and approves the SIAFU Chapter applications, creates resources to facilitate and empower the individual SIAFU Chapters, including coordinating the SIAFU Network website, forum, and newsletters. Its primary function is to facilitate communication and contact among the sites and do all it can to strengthen and empower Chapters where they meet.

MEMBERSHIP AND TITLES AND DUTIES OF
SIAFU CHAPTER OFFICERS (LEADERSHIP COUNCIL)

Part of the way to train leadership in your Chapter is to assign roles to different folk within your Chapter where they can lead, and then help them to know how to fulfill that role. A SIAFU Chapter operates with a Leadership Council consisting of four Officer roles: President, Vice President, Secretary, and Treasurer. The Council also has two Support roles related to hosting Chapter meetings and running service projects: Host/Hostess and Service Project Coordinator, respectively.

Before we discuss the various roles of leaders of a SIAFU Chapter, we need to underscore a few general principles concerning their function:

- Individuals join SIAFU Chapters by affirming their personal faith in Jesus Christ, their commitment to SIAFU's mission and vision and its rules, policies, and Statement of Faith, and agree to submit to the Chapter's Leadership Council.

- Candidate members should be publicly affirmed in a charge given to them by the President during a Chapter meeting, where they become official members of the Chapter (see Appendix for *SIAFU Member Charge*).

- All officers and leaders serve under the blessing and endorsement of the church pastor or ministry director.

- Officers and leaders are elected for one-year terms, by simple majority vote of the Chapter members.

- All activities, projects, and programs of any SIAFU Chapter must be subject to the approval of the pastor/ministry director of the sponsoring church or ministry.

Again, members of a SIAFU Chapter must be professing Christians, and Officers and Support Role leaders are to be selected annually by majority vote of the members present, with the pastor's or spiritual authority's blessing and imprimatur (endorsement).

PRESIDENT

The Chapter President serves at the behest of, as liaison of, and under the authority of the pastor/leader of the church and/or ministry. Essentially, the pastor/ministry leader should be regarded as an ex officio member of all SIAFU meetings, i.e., they can attend all meetings, whether planning or sponsored, of the SIAFU Chapter or its Leadership Council. The President will call and chair the SIAFU Chapter Leadership Council and provide general communication to the pastor and the members of the Chapter about its ongoing business and operations.

The President is required to communicate with the pastor/ministry director regarding proposed projects of the Chapter, securing the pastor's blessing to proceed. S/he also should ensure that the Chapter conforms to the doctrine of the church, and to SIAFU Chapter guidelines. The President will preside over the Chapter meetings, opening and closing each meeting, and ensuring that the one-hour-and-fifteen-minute time limit for the meeting is held to consistently. S/he will open the meeting with a welcome of all Chapter attendees. The president will offer or select someone to provide the devotion for each Chapter meeting and will select the person who will lead the worship time for the week.

Vice President

Serves as assistant to the president and takes responsibility for the Chapter meetings in the president's absence. Also, the vice president should preside over Council meetings, when and if the president is absent. The VP role is to provide support for the President and ensure that the decisions of the President and affairs of the Chapter are carried out, in terms of the Chapter meetings, as well as all other Chapter business. The Vice President should be able and ready to step into the President role, if and whenever necessary.

Secretary

The Secretary of the Chapter will manage the records, paperwork, and membership aspect of the Chapter. S/he will keep the list of all the official SIAFU Chapter members and provide reporting on membership, when called upon. The Secretary will keep record of Leadership Council meetings, providing the official minutes for review, and summarize conversations had within the meeting. S/he will note the decisions made and assignments given, and when called upon will communicate to Chapter members regarding Chapter business in between meetings, (e.g., changes in schedule or meeting locations, cancellations, etc.) S/he will also handle all communication with TUMI headquarters, such as questions, online testimonies, suggestions, and pictures.

Treasurer

The Treasurer of the Chapter is charged with managing and overseeing the finances and resources of the Chapter, including (but not limited to) collecting funds for specific events or projects, keeping track of Chapter expenses and funds, and reporting on finances of the Chapter to Chapter leadership, to Chapter members, and to church/ministry leaders. The

Treasurer should be prepared to provide regular, detailed reports of the Chapter's financial status to its members.

HOST/HOSTESS

This role applies to each regular Chapter gathering. The Host/Hostess should ensure that the meeting room is clean and set up before each Chapter meeting; cleaned up afterward; trash taken out and room left in better shape than when the meeting started. S/he should also coordinate snacks, set out meeting refreshments, and put away food afterward. Finally, the Host/Hostess should enlist the help of volunteers after the meeting to clean up and arrange the room as they found it.

SERVICE PROJECT COORDINATOR

This can be either a roving role, i.e., each service project can have a different Service Project Coordinator, or a Chapter can have a single Service Project Coordinator to coordinate all the projects for a given period of time. The Service Project Coordinator should research and select service projects for the Chapter. S/he should work with the Treasurer for necessary project funds and coordinate service project at the location(s) of project. S/he should also assign someone to take photos of project and get photos to the Vice President.

A SIMPLE STRUCTURE TO ALLOW FOR GREATEST FREEDOM AND MAXIMUM IMPACT

Members of a SIAFU Chapter must be professing Christians who affirm the commitment to the SIAFU Chapter, its doctrine and policies, and its leadership team. The Chapter leadership structure (four Officers and two Support Leaders) is shared by all the SIAFU Chapters throughout the entire national Network. It is not meant to hinder your vision, but to strengthen the possibility of allowing urban disciples to exercise leadership in their local church communities.

Of course, on the start of your SIAFU Chapter, you may only have a handful of members, perhaps not even enough members of the Chapter to account for all the Officers and support leaders! Be flexible and open to the Lord; do what you can to start, but be open to filling out these positions as God brings more members into your Chapter. We are confident that, with God's blessing and help, your Chapter will grow in number and strength, and this growth will more and more require good order, clear records, and open dialogue over all matters in the Chapter. Identifying, equipping, and releasing urban disciples for leadership is precisely what the SIAFU Network is about!

Please note: It is important to restate that these positions and the SIAFU Chapter itself are under the authority and blessing of the pastor or spiritual authority in a particular church or organization that is sponsoring the Chapter. *Under no circumstances can a Chapter operate without the pastor or spiritual authority's blessing (chaplain, director, etc.).* No Chapter can function on its own; it must be connected to a local assembly or organization whose pastor and spiritual authority has endorsed its work.

FOR CHAPTERS ON THE INSIDE

All of the information contained in pages 89-93 (i.e., references to leadership functions, financial requirements, and contact information) are related only to volunteers outside the institution, or to those individuals who are granted authority by the authorized jail/prison officials. Each SIAFU Chapter absolutely must conduct its activities in accordance with all prison/jail requirements, no exceptions allowed.

In light of this, Chapters on the inside cannot use the leadership offices or require strict membership compliance as in a Chapter's normal operation. This is forbidden as it is most likely against the policy of most Departments of Corrections to allow any one inmate to have leadership or authority over another. Even with these necessary limitations, however, you can allow different regular attendees of the Chapter to read Scripture, lead worship, help set up for the meeting, or clean up afterward, etc. The responsibilities of a Chapter meeting can be delegated among members without the need for any of these roles in pages 89-93.

In the extremely rare cases where jail/prison authorities allow the sponsoring church to permit some form of SIAFU responsibilities to be given to inmates, the outside church must retain the ongoing responsibilities of its own Chapter.

HOSTING SIAFU NETWORK CHAPTER MEETINGS:
HINTS AND SUGGESTIONS

OPENLY WELCOME, ENCOURAGE, AND CHALLENGE CITY PEOPLE TO BECOME DISCIPLES IN CHRIST

A SIAFU Chapter meeting is an assembly of urban Christians who seek to help and challenge one another in their spiritual journey in Christ. The regular meeting of the SIAFU Chapter is the key to the strength of our national network; we are a national fellowship of men and women who strive to welcome all true believers in Christ and equip them through prayer, testimony, and friendship to fulfill God's will for their lives. We desire to make these gatherings open and fresh, a safe place where we can challenge fellow Christians to live the Christian life, or invite friends, neighbors, and associates to become followers of Jesus.

Why do we need SIAFU Chapter Meetings?

1. *Our meetings can be places of **welcome and belonging**, where non-believers can hear the Good News, and Christians can be encouraged in their faith.* SIAFU gatherings are meetings where urban disciples can encourage and inspire one another. (Rom. 15.4-7 – "Whatever was written in former days was written for our instruction, that through endurance and through the encouragement of the Scriptures we might have hope. May the God of endurance and encouragement grant you to live in such harmony with one another, in accord with Christ Jesus, that together you may with one voice glorify the God and Father of our Lord Jesus Christ. Therefore welcome one another as Christ has welcomed you, for the glory of God.")

2. *Our meetings can be times where we **challenge and exhort** each other to abandon all for Christ, striving to live as disciples of Jesus where we are.* SIAFU gatherings offer opportunity for urban Christians to "stir up" each other to live as disciples of Christ, and to bear witness of the Lord in their lives and communities. (Heb. 10.24-25 – "And let us consider how to stir up one another to love and good works, not

neglecting to meet together, as is the habit of some, but encouraging one another, and all the more as you see the Day drawing near.")

3. *Our meetings can be places where we **organize service projects** in our communities that meet needs and transform our neighborhoods for the Kingdom.* SIAFU gatherings can become ministry incubators, allowing local urban Christians to do good works on behalf of others in the neighborhoods where they meet. (Phil. 1.27 – "Only let your manner of life be worthy of the gospel of Christ, so that whether I come and see you or am absent, I may hear of you that you are standing firm in one spirit, with one mind striving side by side for the faith of the gospel.")

FOR CHAPTERS ON THE INSIDE

This is also the case for Chapters inside Prison walls. Chapters on the inside will need to function more as a Christian "call out" within the prison or jail, a gathering that is sponsored by your church or ministry. This will provide both an opportunity to encourage our Christian brothers and sisters who are in the facility as well as share our testimonies of faith with those who attend who may not yet know Christ.

Remember, your church- or ministry-sponsored SIAFU Chapter will be under the authority of the corrections facility. Although you should be free to minister to and encourage the men or women in your SIAFU Chapter, you have no spiritual authority over them. Continue to encourage, rebuke, exhort, challenge, build up, comfort and teach them but realize that all activities of the SIAFU Chapter fall under the authority of the corrections system of which you are a part.

A PROPOSED SIAFU CHAPTER MEETING STRUCTURE

Plan out your SIAFU Meeting ahead of time each week. All SIAFU Chapter meetings should be planned and operated in the most excellent, disciplined, and deliberate manner! Review the SIAFU *Chapter Meeting Planning Sheet* (found in the Appendix) and complete your *SIAFU Chapter Meeting Worksheet* (also found in the Appendix and on our website at *www.tumi.org/siafu.worksheet*). The key to solid Chapter gatherings is good advanced planning. Select any special participants to lead areas of the Chapter meeting (if desired). The general rule of thumb is clear: leave no detail of a SIAFU Chapter meeting to chance; fill out the SIAFU Meeting Worksheet to plan out each Chapter meeting.

One principle is extremely important in hosting your Chapter meetings. As a rule, plan out your Chapter Meeting, from start to finish, to be no longer than one hour and fifteen minutes total time. Why? First, people will learn to trust the SIAFU Chapter meeting format, making it easier for attendees to understand and predict the gathering times. Next, filling an hour and fifteen minutes with great testimony, song, and prayer will make your Chapter meetings full, with little room for waste or drag. Finally, an hour-and-fifteen-minute-long period will demand that you plan out everything for your meeting; you will probably need to manage your time efficiently.

Of course, while you may wind up going ten or fifteen minutes longer, you want to discipline your time in such a way that, normally, you are done after an hour and fifteen minutes. Those who wish to stay later can do so, once the meeting is finished.

AN HOUR-AND-FIFTEEN-MINUTE TEMPLATE TO GUIDE YOUR CHAPTER MEETING

The following template is a proposed outline for an hour-and-fifteen-minute-long SIAFU Chapter meeting. Feel free to structure your agenda as the Lord leads (all the times are approximate and suggested, and shouldn't be seen as hard and fast demands). The president is responsible for the overall flow of the meeting and should select others and delegate to them responsibility for specific pieces of the Chapter meeting.

1. *Welcome everyone in attendance* in the name of Jesus Christ (5 min). The presider of the meeting should welcome everyone in attendance. Open each Chapter meeting with a warm greeting and offer a brief explanation to everyone present what the SIAFU Network is and what you hope to accomplish together. The presider may elect to read the SIAFU mission statement, so everyone can hear again why you gather, and what your intent together is.

2. *Offer an invocation (opening prayer)* seeking the Lord's blessing and direction for your meeting (3 min). Ask the Lord to come and be present in your meeting, sending the Holy Spirit among you all, leading and directing as you strengthen one another together in testimony, the Word, and prayer.

3. *Spend a brief time in worship and praise* to the Lord together (10 min). Recite together to music the SIAFU Chant, and spend some time singing several songs of worship and praise together.

4. *Allow for testimonies from others* for the sake of encouragement and challenge (typically 3 testimonies of 3-4 minutes each and an open time) (15 min). You may, too, elect before the date of the meeting, to ask someone to give a special testimony, a little longer in length, which relates to the theme of your meeting that week. Follow the leading of the Holy Spirit, thinking clearly of who might share that can edify and encourage the members during the meeting.

   a. Encourage those who give testimonies to be concise, clear, and fresh. They should focus on what they have recently learned from Christ through their experience and be edifying in their topics and expression. Also, these should strive to both encourage and challenge those present to live more fully devoted and committed to Jesus Christ. Merely rehearsing one's faults or sins, or complaining about a situation or person is not offering testimony to what God is doing in one's life. Words should be clearly directed to help others know and love Christ, and as much as possible, strive to build up all who are in attendance.

   b. Please note: *Someone will need to ride shotgun on the giving of the testimonies! In their enthusiasm and excitement, people can easily convert 3-4 minutes to 10-12 minutes, without realizing what they have done to your time! Gently but firmly remind all folk who give testimonies to be aware of the time, and if they wind up going longer, then quietly intervene, asking them to wrap up their comments, so the next person might share.*

5. *Present a biblical challenge from the Word* (e.g., on how to become a Christian, on how to be a better follower/disciple of Christ; on being God's person in family and on the job, etc.) (20 min.). Your challenges should strive to do several things:

   a. Be grounded upon and flow from a specific passage from the Scriptures

   b. Speak directly to the needs, concerns, and issues faced by the members of your SIAFU Chapter

   c. Challenge those in attendance to higher and deeper levels of commitment to Christ and his Kingdom

6. *Spend time together in prayer and supplication for one another* (10 min). Rather than taking much time to share all of the prayer requests that might be present, allow for a minute or two to gather the needs of the group. Then break into smaller units, of four to five people, and pray for the needs shared quickly. Remind them to pray short prayers, directly to the Lord, allowing for everyone present who wishes to pray to intercede for others. After ten minutes, the presider should close out the prayer session from the front, ending the prayer time with a general prayer to the Lord on behalf of all of those present.

   Remember, focused, continuous prayer will be the key to your SIAFU chapter's maturity and growth. Prayer will undergird your efforts and cause you to have great impact on your families and friends, making your service and outreach effective as you follow up on opportunities to represent Christ where you live. TUMI's prayer movement, Let God Arise!, was established in 2000 out of the belief that only God can change the city. Your SIAFU Chapter can sponsor concerts of prayer alongside us and others praying for the revival of the city. Join us as we ask God for our cities' healing and transformation in a passionate and disciplined way on behalf of the unreached urban poor worldwide. God can change the city! You can find a treasure trove of free and effective prayer resources on our site to help you do this. Visit our site at *www.tumi.org/letgodarise*.

7. *Offer a challenge to all of the attendees* to serve or demonstrate their love for Christ in a tangible way (2 min.). End each meeting with a specific challenge to each of the disciples to demonstrate tangibly their allegiance to Christ in a practical, specific way this week. For instance, they could go and speak to their spouses, children, and relatives a word of encouragement and thanksgiving, they could offer to do extra work for a coworker on the job, volunteer to do a chore in their home outside the norm. Whatever they decide, we should remind them that the SIAFU Network is a network committed to servant leadership, to practical, good works that are demonstrated in the midst of our lives – our homes, marriages, families, jobs, churches, and neighborhoods. Never have a Chapter meeting without committing to go away and doing something that week!

8. *Provide a short briefing with announcements* on Chapter business (7 min). For example, you can give info on an upcoming work project and details, and remind people of the opportunity to give to support Chapter expenses (i.e., monies that go toward upcoming work projects, meeting expenses like coffee). Give information about your next SIAFU meeting, and warmly invite folk to hang around as long as they would like after the meeting for fellowship and refreshments.

9. *Offer a benediction to the Lord at the conclusion of your gathering* (3 min). Have someone ask God's blessing on those present as they depart and scatter to their various homes and life situations. Invite those who do not know the Lord to come to him, and affirm the truth with all who are present. Follow the Spirit's leading, and always challenge them to live as disciples of Christ until you gather again. After the prayer, officially end the SIAFU Chapter meeting.

10. *Wrap up the meeting with clean up and closing the meeting* (post-meeting). After you have hosted your Chapter meeting, get volunteers to help clean up and arrange the room as you found it. Record any monies members gave for the support of the group, and make sure that someone will write up notes regarding any Chapter business decided during the meeting.

SIAFU Chapter Meeting Worksheet
(One-hour-and-fifteen-minute template)

1. **(5 min.) Welcome in the name of Jesus Christ**
   Person's name: _____
   a. Greeting
   b. Affirmation of the SIAFU Network's mission and vision
   c. Acknowledgment of visitors
   d. Asking cell phones to be disabled during meeting

2. **(3 min.) Invocation (opening prayer)**
   Person's name: _____

3. **(10 min.) Worship and praise**
   Leader's name: _____
   a. SIAFU Chant Leader: _____
   b. Worship song #1: _____
   c. Worship song #2: _____
   d. Worship song #3: _____

4. **(15 min.) Testimonies**
   Person's name: _____
   a. Testimony #1: _____
   b. Testimony #2: _____
   c. Testimony #3: _____

5. **(20 min.) Biblical exhortation**
   Person's name: _____

6. **(10 min.) Prayer and supplication**
   Person's name: _____

7. **(3 min.) Specific Chapter challenge**
   Person's name: _____

8. **(6 min.) Briefing and announcements**
   Person's name: _____

9. **(3 min.) Benediction and closing prayer**
   Person's name: _____

10. **(Till done) Wrap up and clean up**
    Person's name: _____

HANDLE ONGOING CHAPTER AFFAIRS WITH EXCELLENCE

As you host your gatherings, you will need to make certain that you stay on top of the various business and affairs of the Chapter. This is the responsibility of the officers and leaders of every SIAFU Chapter.

1. *Keep good records of all SIAFU business.* Collect, record, and handle money weekly, keeping careful track of expenses and income. Report to your members on a monthly basis what has been received and what expenditures there might be for an upcoming project.

2. *Communicate with members regularly and clearly.* The officers should make sure that members are kept abreast of all Chapter business and issues, from the location of the next meeting, to the date of the next election of officers. Collecting phone numbers and e-mails is helpful, and a good way to write and inform all interested parties on upcoming Chapter happenings and events.

3. *Plan out your service projects well.* Determine what needs to be done for upcoming service projects, what announcements need to be made this week (e.g., what the project is, administrative details for this project – time, location, what to wear, what to bring, how long we will be working at this project; if over lunch, what we will do for lunch, etc.).

MANAGING YOUR CHAPTER RESOURCES:
HANDLING FINANCES AND GOODS

Good stewardship and integrity requires proper accountability when it comes to handling money. Below are a few important principles to think about as you decide how your chapter will handle its funds. The key is to think through all matters related to your resources, draft a sound plan of managing those resources, and then follow the plan, reviewing later how things went. Here are a few elements that should be a part of your plan.

1. Adopt clear, transparent, and open written procedures regarding all monies and resources. Form policies that are helpful. For instance, if you start a bank account, make sure that the person who writes the checks cannot sign them! The treasurer should cross-train someone to do what he does, so there is always another person who can conduct business for the Chapter, under the president's instruction. It should be a policy that no one who drafts checks can sign them to themselves. Always include more than one person in counting Chapter funds. Simple, common-sense policies like this will ensure that your business is conducted responsibly and rightly.

2. Decide the stream/flow of your monies. In other words, what people will count and collect it after the meetings? Where will you deposit the money, once collected? How will you maintain records of your funds, and how often will you report those findings to the Chapter? Do you intend to provide receipts for donations?

3. Decide how monies will be dispersed. Once you have a sound way of managing your funds (even if they are small!), how will you create a process to spend these funds? Who will make the financial decisions to use Chapter funds for Chapter business? How will you report to the Chapter how funds are spent, and where?

ENCOURAGE SIAFU MEMBERS AND FRIENDS TO SUPPORT THE CHAPTER FINANCIALLY

The question of resources is directly related to the church or ministry that sponsors the SIAFU Chapter. We encourage you to offer the opportunity for Chapter members to give to the support of the Chapter every week. The funds collected should be shared with the sponsoring church or ministry, to cover their expenses for hosting the Chapter. Whenever possible, the Chapter should bless the sponsoring church or ministry with resources or service, all in the name of the Lord. While there may be a variety of Chapter expenses, it is truly important for Chapter members to contribute funds to help with those expenses, as they can and as they desire.

The critical issue regarding money, especially for the sponsoring church or organization, will be the independence of the SIAFU Chapter. In other words, as much as possible, each Chapter should strive to be self-sufficient financially for its own activities and expenses. The members of the Chapter may sponsor projects to raise funds to cover expenses, but great care should be given to ensure that the pastor and/or authority of the sponsoring organization knows of your projects and possesses a full and clear account of what monies are being raised, why you need them, and where they are to be spent. We have challenged every Chapter in the network to be sensitive and responsible to support and acknowledge their sponsoring church or organization. Due diligence should be done by all involved to ensure that, on the one hand, the Chapter strives in all activities to pay its own bills for any outstanding debts. On the other hand, the Chapter should also strive to support the sponsoring church, helping out in every way with funds and resources to strengthen the church's ministry and work.

FOR CHAPTERS ON THE INSIDE

Please note that any reference to financial handling, requirements, or organization is strictly subject to the rules and demands of the sponsoring jail or prison. Each SIAFU chapter must conduct all of its activities in accordance with all prison/jail requirements. Ensure that you make no decisions connected to anything related to finances without hearing the policies of the jail/prison officials, and once learned, strictly comply with their demands without exception.

CREATED FOR GOOD WORKS:
SPONSORING A SIAFU PROJECT

One of the most important elements in the SIAFU Network is each Chapter's commitment to demonstrate good works through its members and friends. In every community and neighborhood in the city, there are dozens of wholesome, practical, and helpful projects which can be done to demonstrate the justice and peace of the Kingdom. Each Chapter, in becoming one within the Network, makes a commitment to doing tangible, practical works of service within their neighborhood – projects which can reveal to others our love for Christ and for them.

Many of these service projects, once clarified and organized, can be done at little to no cost to your team if you utilize what everyone has available to them (e.g. paint brushes, brooms, hauling trash, garden tools, lawn mower, rakes). For those service projects that will require some investment on the Chapter's part, you may want to consider having a fund raiser or ask for donations to help you support this project. Here are some practical tips to help you think through your service projects:

1. Look at possible projects based on time, skill level of team, number of team members, and decide on a project that best works for your team (with the approval of your leaders).

2. Keep clear lines of communication open. Make sure that you contact the person or persons you will be doing this project on behalf of, and take careful notes on what precisely your Chapter will do, along with all the specifics of the project.

3. Communicate all the details of the upcoming service project description to your Chapter volunteer team members so they can get it on their calendars and make arrangements to attend with any tools or goods they will need to participate.

4. Write out all tasks that need to be done for this project. Based on the tasks, make a list of resources that you will need. Make sure that if some team members can supply any of these, that you contact them and see if they are willing to use their resources for the project.

5. Create a budget for that project based on those items. Secure all necessary supplies and resources you will need to accomplish the project, and double check that you will have them for the day or dates of the event.

6. Plan refreshments for the team, and arrange for parts of the team to prep the work area, purchase any necessary items, and bring snacks to the service project.

7. Appoint one of the Chapter members to take pictures throughout this service project (and get you all of the digital files when the project is done).

8. Finalize arrival time, work time, and any directions that will need to be covered with the particular client of the service project, and communicate this information to all chapter members who will participate before the project begins.

9. Conduct and do the service project together as a Chapter – excellently, carefully, and thoroughly for the Lord.

10. After the project is completed, clean up the work area neatly, and put everything away. Remove all litter and trash left at the project (if applicable), and ensure that the workspace looks better than when you arrived.

11. Later, evaluate how the Chapter volunteers worked together, and celebrate the results of the project with the team. The best timing will usually be within a week or two after you have completed the project. Make sure that you file any necessary paperwork and plans you came up with for this service project (for future reference, in case you decide to repeat this kind of project again).

FOR CHAPTERS ON THE INSIDE

Because of the special conditions of the incarcerated and the rules and regulations of each jail or prison facility, all SIAFU service projects must be shared and cleared by the appropriate correction officials. Each institution will determine and set the limits of such kind of sponsored event (or even whether such a project is permissible), and each Chapter inside must be careful to comply to all constraints and permissions that apply. Please check our website, *www.tumi.org/siafu* for service project ideas for Chapters on the Inside.

Go with God:
How to Keep Your SIAFU Chapter in Good Shape and Good Standing

In order to ensure that your Chapter continues to grow and prosper, you will need to make sure that you set some time apart for planning and review. The Holy Spirit will give you insight and direction as your Chapter continues to encourage, challenge, and serve urban disciples. A little forethought, prayer, brainstorming, and effort can go a long way in making sure that your Chapter continues to grow, both in number and influence.

1. *Set aside time to set goals for the upcoming year.* Make time as officers and leaders to get together and brainstorm goals for your Chapter. Clarify together your mission, what you believe God wants you to do in the next twelve months.

    a. Look at the critical needs, how they are being met, and what you can do to make a difference together. Set goals together on what you want to get done, in terms of the results you want.

    b. Select those priorities you believe God wants you to accomplish now, and share these with the Chapter members. Outline step-by-step strategies for each important goal, outline projects, and make plans to accomplish them.

    c. Trust God to lead you as the year unfolds, and always take time to pray and evaluate together what you see, and how God is working. The Holy Spirit will guide you as you move forward, pursuing those things that you believe God wants you to accomplish this upcoming year.

2. *Meet regularly as a Chapter Council (Leadership Council) to keep track of Chapter business.* The Officers (president, vice president, secretary, and treasurer) of the Chapter should meet regularly (once each

month, minimum) to plan out Chapter business, address ongoing issues, and review progress toward its goals. The more you can get together to prayerfully consider what is happening and what you believe God wants you to do, the better and more effective your Chapter will be.

3. *Stay in touch with communication from TUMI International.* Read carefully the regular e-mails and newsletters that you will receive, and stay informed of all the upcoming retreats, conferences, and service ideas we provide, including all SIAFU Blog and published resources.

4. *Communicate what God is doing with other Chapters in the Network.* You can easily upload your photos and stories every quarter to the SIAFU Network headquarters online. The SIAFU website is a great resource to expose your Chapter to others who are doing great things for the Lord, and will be a ready resource to provide you with additional testimonies, videos, and photos of amazing things God is doing. You also will be able to harvest great ideas for your Chapter meetings and service projects, and find practical ideas to encourage and challenge those in your Chapter to go on with the Lord.

5. *Be sure to renew your annual membership.* The renewal process is simple and affordable. You can renew your membership each year as a SIAFU Chapter by simply reviewing and affirming the SIAFU Statement of Faith, paying the annual renewal fee of $25, and confirming your church or ministry's continued sponsorship of your Chapter.

6. *Access TUMI's resources to edify and equip your SIAFU Chapter members.* Remember, many resources exist to strengthen you as you lead and expand your Chapter's numbers and influence:

    a. *The SIAFU Network Guidebook*: this one-stop guidebook provides all you need to establish your SIAFU Chapter

b. *SIAFU Chapter Meeting Guide*: a handy resource for chapter leaders to organize their chapter meetings

c. *The SIAFU Network Website (www.tumi.org/siafu)*: SIAFU's online storehouse filled with numerous aids for your Chapter, with info to connect your Chapter to the entire network of SIAFU Chapters across the country (and around the world)

d. *The SIAFU Chapter Resource Kit*: a must-have toolbox for every SIAFU Chapter, including:

- One official, embossed SIAFU Certificate printed with your Chapter Name (for approved SIAFU Chapters)

- One additional *SIAFU Network Guidebook*

- Two *SIAFU Network Chapter Meeting Guides*

- One *Let God Arise! Prayer Booklet* with a pack of ten brochures

- Twenty SIAFU Network brochures

- One copy of the *Mo' Power* Spiritual Warfare Series CD (which contains a digital studio mixed version of the *SIAFU Chant*)

- One 24" x 36" SIAFU poster

e. *Suggested Service Projects*: a constantly updated list of potential service projects that your SIAFU Chapter can do to show Christ's love to your church and/or community

f. *Listing of SIAFU Events and Conferences*: SIAFU-sponsored events and conferences provide opportunities for worship, networking, service, and partnership among Chapters

g. Resources for discipleship and leadership

(1) *Fit to Represent: The Vision for Discipleship Seminar*: TUMI's attempt to raise up a new generation of qualified spiritual

laborers who will catch the passion to invest in others for the sake of the Church and Christ's Kingdom

(2) *The Sacred Roots Follow-Up Curriculum*: a biblical and practical follow-up course for new and growing Christians in the city

(3) *Jesus Cropped from the Picture: Why Christians Get Bored and How to Restore Them to Vibrant Faith* (by Don Allsman): an insightful commentary on the problem of why Christians get bored and how to overcome it

(4) *Sacred Roots: A Primer on the Great Tradition*: an overview of the foundation of Christian faith and practice, and how we can renew our contemporary faith

(5) *Get Up and Go: Lessons in Freedom and the Power to Produce* (by Daniel Davis): a look at creative freedom through the lens of punk culture, and what it can teach disciples of Christ today on how to live free for Christ

(6) *Let God Arise! Prayer Booklet and Prayer Brochure*: a challenging prayer booklet issuing a call to people to intercede on behalf of the healing and transformation of the cities of America and the world

(7) *TUMI Art and Prints*: a wide array of beautiful and affordable Christian art available for purchase today

(8) *The Foundations for Ministry Series*: informative and inspiring Bible studies on various topics designed for personal and small group use

(9) *The Most Amazing Story Ever Told*: a booklet explaining the wonder and power of the Christian story for city Christians

(10) *Once Upon a Time*: brochure and poster of the entire Christian Story

7. If you absolutely need, for some reason, to contact us here at TUMI, please use the following web and e-mail addresses:

   a. You may contact us at TUMI International through our SIAFU Coordinator, *siafucoordinator@tumi.org*.

   b. SIAFU Chapters: All of our SIAFU Chapters and Chapter Coordinators are listed on our website at *www.tumi.org/siafu*. As new Chapters are started, their contact information will be posted on our site. Check this often to see what other Chapters are located in your area.

APPENDIX

THE SIAFU NETWORK
APPLICATION FOR CHAPTER ADMISSION
A digital version of this form can be found at *www.tumi.org/siafu.application*

PERSONAL INFORMATION

Name (First, Middle, Last)	
Home address	
City, State, ZIP	
E-mail address	Date of birth
Home phone	Sex ☐ Male ☐ Female
Cell phone	Marital status ☐ Single ☐ Married

How long have you been a Christian?

CHURCH INFORMATION

What is the name of the church you attend?

What is the name of your Pastor?

Does your church have a denominational affiliation (Baptist, Presbyterian, Methodist, non-denomination, etc.)?

Are you a member of this church? If so, for how long?

What is your role in y our church, if any?

A SIAFU CHAPTER IN YOUR CHURCH OR MINISTRY, OR A CHAPTER ON THE INSIDE

1. How did you hear about SIAFU?

2. Where do you wish to start a SIAFU Chapter? If you wish to extend your SIAFU Chapter meetings in a jail or a prison, what is its name, and what is its contact information?

3. Why do you want to start a SIAFU Chapter in your church or organization?

4. In your opinion, how do you believe a SIAFU Chapter will strengthen and build up your church/ministry?

5. In your judgment, how does one actually become a Christian, and what does it mean to live as a disciple of Christ?

6. List three areas where you have seen genuine change in your life since becoming a Christian, and what did God provide to help you grow in these areas?

7. Describe your discussion with your pastor/ministry leader about your desire to start a SIAFU Chapter in your church. How did they react, and did they grant you permission to go forward with forming one there? What, if any, concerns did they have about sponsoring a Chapter in their church/organization?

8. In what ways do you think that a SIAFU Chapter may strengthen the leadership in your church or organization?

9. How can you avoid conflicts of interest between the Chapter and your sponsoring church or organization? In other words, how will you work to make sure that all communication is clear and open with your leaders about your Chapter?

10. SIAFU Chapters will be made up of differing backgrounds and religious traditions. Are you willing to relate to others in the SIAFU Network? Why or why not?

11. How many people does your church or organization serve on a monthly basis?

12. Have you read and do you agree with World Impact's Affirmation of Faith? (see following pages)
    ☐ Yes   ☐ No

WORLD IMPACT'S AFFIRMATION OF FAITH STATEMENT

As a ministry of *World Impact*, *The Urban Ministry Institute* unequivocally endorses *World Impact's* Affirmation of Faith statement expressing our allegiance to the orthodox faith.

There is one living and true God, infinitely perfect in glory, wisdom, holiness, justice, power and love, one in His essence but eternally existing in three persons: God the Father, God the Son and God the Holy Spirit. God sovereignly created the world out of nothing, so that His creation, while wholly dependent upon Him, neither comprises part of God, nor conditions His essential perfection.

The books which form the canon of the Old and New Testaments are verbally inspired by God, inerrant in the original writings, the only infallible rule of faith and practice.

God created humankind in His own image, in a state of original righteousness, from which humankind subsequently fell by a voluntary revolt, and consequently is guilty, inherently corrupt and subject to divine wrath.

Jesus Christ, the eternal Son, became man without ceasing to be God by uniting to His divine nature a true human nature in His incarnation, and so continues to be both God and man, in two distinct natures and one person, forever. He was conceived by the Holy Spirit, born of the virgin Mary, exhibited His deity by manifold miracles, fulfilled the requirements of the Law by His sinless life, shed His blood as a vicarious and propitiatory atonement for humankind's sin, was resurrected from the dead in the same body, now glorified. He ascended into heaven and now intercedes in glory for His redeemed as our great high priest and advocate, and as the Head of the Church and Lord of the individual believer.

The Holy Spirit convicts the world of sin, righteousness and judgment, through the ministry of regeneration and sanctification applies salvation and places believers into the Church, guides and comforts God's children, indwells, directs, gifts and empowers the Church in godly living and service in order to fulfill the Great Commission, and seals and keeps the believer until Christ returns.

Every person, regardless of race or rank, who receives the Lord Jesus Christ by faith is born into the family of God and receives eternal life. This occurs solely because of the grace of God and has no ground in human merit.

The Holy Church is the one institution specifically ordained of God to function in the furthering of the Kingdom until Christ comes again. It consists of all those regenerated by the Spirit of God, in mystical union and communion both with Christ, the head of the Body, and with fellow believers. Neighborhood congregations are the local manifestation of the Church universal. In obedience to the command of Christ, these congregations preach the word of God, equip God's people for the work of ministry, and administer the Lord's Supper and Baptism.

The Lord Jesus Christ will return bodily, visibly and personally to receive His own, to conform believers to His own image and to establish His millennial kingdom. He will judge the quick and the dead and will effect a final separation of the redeemed and the lost, assigning unbelievers to eternal punishment and believers to eternal glory, enjoying conscious fellowship with Him.

Humankind's chief end in life is to honor and glorify Almighty God. Personal salvation is a means to this end.

THE SIAFU NETWORK
PASTOR'S REFERENCE FORM
A digital version of this form can be found at *www.tumi.org/siafu.reference*

_____has applied to begin a SIAFU Chapter (and become the coordinator of that Chapter) of *The Urban Ministry Institute* (TUMI) in your congregation. As all SIAFU Chapters must be hosted in a church or ministry, the pastor's approval is a necessary part of the acceptance. The applicant has, therefore, given your name as a reference. Each applicant must submit a recommendation from his/her pastor (or spiritual authority, if the candidate is starting a Chapter in an organization other than a local church). This recommendation is given serious attention; therefore, we request that you complete the form carefully and candidly, and return it directly to: *siafu@tumi.org* or mail it to:

> The Urban Ministry Institute, SIAFU Coordinator
> 3701 E. 13th St.
> Wichita KS 67208.

---

1. What is your name?

2. How long have you known the applicant?

3. How well do you know him/her?
   - ❑ Just by name
   - ❑ A few personal contacts
   - ❑ Fairly well
   - ❑ Close, ongoing relationship

4. To the best of your knowledge, has the applicant been born again by faith in Jesus Christ?
   - ❑ Yes
   - ❑ No
   - ❑ I don't know

5. How involved is the applicant in the activities and outreach of your church?
   - ❑ Irregular attendance, little interest in your church's activities or outreach ministries
   - ❑ Seldom participates in your church's activities or outreach, but is a regular attender
   - ❑ Is cooperative and is usually willing to help in your church's activities and outreach ministries
   - ❑ Enthusiastically engages in your church's activities and outreach ministries

6. In what areas of your church's life and ministry has the applicant been regularly active?

7. In what areas of your church's life and ministry has the applicant shown leadership abilities?

8. In your opinion, what spiritual gifts and/or special abilities does this applicant possess?

9. In comparison with other members of your church, how would you rate this person in the following areas?

Area	Outstanding	Above Average	Average	Below Average	Don't Know
Leadership					
Dependability					
Honesty					
Teachability					
Initiative					
Judgment					
Relationships with Others					
Loyalty to Church					
Knowledge of Scripture					

10. Is the applicant's overall character such that you would be confident in recommending him/her to lead others? (Please include any additional remarks you may have.)

11. Has the applicant talked to you about his/her desire to start a SIAFU Chapter in your church? Are you supportive of this desire? (Please include any additional remarks you may have.)

12. How would you describe the applicant's role in your church or denomination?
   (Check all that apply.)
   ❏ a senior pastor
   ❏ a deacon
   ❏ a member of your pastoral staff
   ❏ a lay leader
   ❏ a Christian worker
   ❏ a pastoral trainee
   ❏ an elder
   ❏ a teacher or trainer
   ❏ other (please explain):

Signed _____ Date: _____

Position _____ Church Name _____

Church Address and Phone _____

_____

CHAPTER LAUNCH CHECKLIST
A printable version of this form can be found at *www.tumi.org/siafu.checklist*

Determine the mission and focus of Your SIAFU Chapter

□ Determine who this Chapter will be for, that is, who will be invited to attend

□ Figure out if you want to host more than one group in your chapter (e.g. Men, Women, Teens)

□ Decide on your SIAFU Chapter Name

Develop the structure to administrate your Chapter

□ Familiarize yourself with SIAFU website (*www.tumi.org/siafu*)

□ Receive and review the SIAFU Chapter Resource Kit

□ Decide when your Chapter will meet (day and time and how often)

□ Determine how to handle expenses and funds

Secure and organize your Chapter meeting area

□ Determine where you will host your Chapter meetings (get keys if necessary)

□ Secure any necessary equipment you may need for your Chapter meetings (e.g. CD player, overhead projector or TV, DVD player, white board)

Promote your SIAFU Chapter

□ Set up time with your pastor to share with the church about the SIAFU group(s)

□ Talk to others about your SIAFU group (encourage people to invite their friends). *Please note that if there is a TUMI/Prison Fellowship satellite in your area you could get permission to visit the prison during a class and invite students to join your group upon their release.*

Finalize all necessary details and positions for your Chapter

□ Complete the online Chapter Completion Form and submit annual fee (online)

□ Brainstorm list of names for interim President, Vice President, Administrator, Host/Hostess, and Project Coordinator until they can be voted in by actual members and run by pastor for approval

CHAPTER COMPLETION FORM

THE SIAFU NETWORK · THE URBAN MINISTRY INSTITUTE

Please complete this form online at *www.tumi.org/siafu.completion*

CHAPTER INFORMATION

	Chapter State	Chapter Country
Chapter City		
SIAFU Chapter Name		
Chapter Coordinator Name (Dr. Rev. Mr. Mrs. Ms.)		
Chapter Coordinator E-mail address	Chapter Coordinator Phone#	
I would like my phone number listed with our SIAFU Chapter's contact information on the SIAFU Chapter Meetings page on *www.tumi.org/siafu*	❑ Yes ❑ No	

HOST CHURCH OR MINISTRY INFORMATION

Church or Ministry of SIAFU Chapter	Pastor (or Ministry Supervisor) of Church or Ministry
Church or Ministry Address	Phone #
City, State, ZIP	

JAIL OR PRISON EXTENSION INFORMATION

Name of SIAFU Chapter	Name of Chaplain
Jail or Prison Address	Chaplain Phone #
City, State, ZIP	

CHAPTER INFORMATION FOR SIAFU WEBSITE

Name of SIAFU Chapter Meeting Location	Day and Time of meetings, if known
Address	
City, State, ZIP	

❑   I have read and agree with the SIAFU Network's (World Impact's) Statement of Faith

CHAPTER START-UP FEE

❑	1 - 50 individuals served monthly	$50
❑	51 - 100 individuals served monthly	$75
❑	101 - 250 individuals served monthly	$100
❑	251+ individuals served monthly	$150

The one-time* Chapter start-up fee is calculated on a sliding fee scale based on the approximate number of individuals your church or organization serves on a monthly basis. This is an honor system; whatever estimate you provide will be accepted, and you can then pay the fee associated with your guestimate. See the scale, left, and check the box that best describes your Chapter.

* Please note, there is an annual Chapter renewal fee of $25 along with your continued affirmation of our Statement of Faith (due January 31 after the first full year of membership).

SAMPLE SIAFU CHAPTER BUDGET
FORECASTING YOUR CHAPTER'S YEARLY EXPENSES

We provide this sample SIAFU Chapter budget (see next page) to stir your imagination on the kinds of expenses you will have during the course of your year. Some of these items, of course, can be obtained for less expense, and not all of the budget categories will apply to every Chapter. Still, having an overall annual budget plan for your Chapter will not only help you to avoid surprises month by month, but also pinpoint for you the kinds of funds you'll need to carry out your activities and projects as you go. (You can adjust your budget based on what you need, and what categories will apply to your Chapter). Your Leadership Council should spend time forecasting your goals for the year and set your budget based on the various events and desires you hope to accomplish at your Chapter.

SAMPLE ANNUAL BUDGET

* Please note, encourage chapter members to be generous and bring snacks to help with the overall costs of hosting chapter meetings.

Paper products (e.g. cups, plates, stir sticks) ($10/mo)	$120.00
Coffee supplies (coffee, sugar, creamer, etc) ($15/month)	$180.00
Snack purchases* (e.g. popcorn, chips, etc.) ($15/month)	$180.00
Trash bags and cleaning supplies ($10/month)	$120.00
Utility costs (if applicable) ($25/month)	$400.00
Chapter Meeting Guide (for each person who leads Chapter Meetings) 5 @ $5	$25.00
Let God Arise! Prayer Booklets and brochures for each member 10 @ $6	$60.00
SIAFU brochures (to hand out) 50	$38.00
SIAFU display	$230.00
SIAFU poster	$18.00
TUMI art (5-22x28 prints @ $30 each)	$150.00
Frames for 22x28 prints, 5 @ $25 each	$125.00
Quarterly SIAFU meal* (meat/buns for 25 folk x 4 meetings)	$150.00
Quarterly Service Projects ($150 ea, for paint, supplies, rental equipment drinks, snacks, etc.)	$600.00
	———
Sample Budget Total	$2396.00
Chapter Start-up Fee	$50-150.00

(This is a one-time expense based on a sliding scale. See Chapter Completion Form in Appendix for details.)

Annual Chapter Renewal Fee	$25.00

* We encourage you to host SIAFU gatherings for meals, providing the meat/buns and have members bring side dishes and desserts for the meal. The estimate given here is for brats and buns.

SIAFU CHAPTER MEETING
PLANNING SHEET

The following is a summary of the items that need to be assigned/handled at each Chapter meeting. For details on each assignment, please refer to *Part III, Hosting SIAFU Network Chapter Meetings: Hints and Suggestions.* On the following page you will find a worksheet that can be completed with the responsible person for each task. (This form can also be found on our website, *www.tumi.org/siafu.worksheet.*)

1. Determine who will preside over the meeting (open and close meeting, welcoming attendees, ensure that the one-hour-fifteen-minute time limit for the meeting is held to) and ask them to do so.

2. Assign someone to give the Invocation (opening prayer) for the Chapter Meeting.

3. Select songs for the week, print copies of worship songs for attendees, ask others to participate in helping to facilitate (play an instrument, sing, etc.) or lead worship.

4. Contact three Chapter members and ask them to share a word of testimony at the upcoming Chapter meeting. (Make sure you tell them the topic for sharing, and the time limit given.)

5. Appoint or assign someone to present a biblical exhortation for the meeting. (Remember to give any time allotments to the person sharing the Word.)

6. Ask someone to facilitate small group prayer, spending time interceding for each other. (Remind the folk to pray short prayers allowing for everyone who wishes to pray to intercede for others.)

7. Assign and/or ask someone to give the specific Chapter challenge (i.e., a specific Word to encourage and challenge the Chapter, connected to the teaching).

8. Gather and put together announcements, especially those regarding any details of an upcoming service project (e.g., the time of the project, its location, what to bring).

9. Assign someone to the Benediction for the Chapter Meeting, the closing prayers for the time. (Remember any significant prayer requests at this time.)

10. Make sure that snacks and drinks will be purchased and prepared for the meeting, and set up well in advance of the meeting.

11. Ensure someone is assigned to unlock and prep the meeting room for the SIAFU Chapter meeting (i.e., that the thermostat is set, chairs set up, the room is clean, and tables are set up, wiped off, and ready for use), and in charge of clean up after the meeting.

SIAFU Chapter Meeting Worksheet
One-Hour-and-Fifteen-Minute Template
A printable version of this form can be found at *www.tumi.org/siafu.worksheet*

1. **(5 min.) Welcome in the name of Jesus Christ**
   Person's name: _____
   a. Greeting
   b. Affirmation of the SIAFU Network's mission and vision
   c. Acknowledgment of visitors
   d. Asking cell phones to be disabled during meeting

2. **(3 min.) Invocation (opening prayer)**
   Person's name: _____

3. **(10 min.) Worship and praise**
   Leader's name: _____
   a. SIAFU Chant Leader: _____
   b. Worship song #1: _____
   c. Worship song #2: _____
   d. Worship song #3: _____

4. **(15 min.) Testimonies**
   Person's name: _____
   a. Testimony #1: _____
   b. Testimony #2: _____
   c. Testimony #3: _____

5. **(20 min.) Biblical exhortation**
   Person's name: _____

6. **(10 min.) Prayer and supplication**
   Person's name: _____

7. **(3 min.) Specific Chapter challenge**
   Person's name: _____

8. **(6 min.) Briefing and announcements**
   Person's name: _____

9. **(3 min.) Benediction and closing prayer**
   Person's name: _____

10. **(Till done) Wrap up and clean up**
    Person's name: _____

SIAFU PROJECT WORKSHEET (FOR SERVICE PROJECTS)

See *Created for Good Works: Sponsoring a SIAFU Project* in Part III of this guidebook for more details.
A printable version of this form can be found at *www.tumi.org/siafu.project*

Service project description: _____

_____

Budget for project: $_____

Contact name/phone for service project: _____

Date, day of week, time, and estimated length (e.g. 4 hrs.) of project: _____

_____

Address (and directions): _____

_____

Tasks to be done for this project:

1. _____
2. _____
3. _____
4. _____
5. _____
6. _____
7. _____
8. _____
9. _____
10. _____

Additional comments:

Resources that Chapter members need to bring:

1. _____
2. _____
3. _____
4. _____
5. _____
6. _____

Items to be purchased for this project (and who will purchase):

1. _____
2. _____
3. _____
4. _____
5. _____
6. _____

Plan and bring refreshments for service project (who?) _____

Photograph service project (who?)

_____

❑ Clean up and remove all trash (team)

❑ Ensure tools are returned to those who brought them, pack up all items that were brought to the service project and put everything away

MEMBERSHIP AND SIAFU LEADERSHIP COUNCIL

CHAPTER OFFICERS: TITLES AND DUTIES

Part of the way to train leadership in your Chapter is to assign roles to different folk within your Chapter where they can lead, and then help them to know how to fulfill that role. A SIAFU Chapter operates with a Leadership Council consisting of four Officer roles: President, Vice President, Secretary, and Treasurer. The Council also has two Support roles related to hosting Chapter meetings and running service projects: Host/Hostess and Service Project Coordinator, respectively.

A SIMPLE STRUCTURE TO ALLOW FOR GREATEST FREEDOM AND MAXIMUM IMPACT

Members of a SIAFU Chapter must be professing Christians who affirm the commitment to the SIAFU Chapter, its doctrine and policies, and its leadership team. The Chapter leadership structure (four Officers and two Support Leaders) is shared by all the SIAFU Chapters throughout the entire national Network. It is not meant to hinder your vision, but to strengthen the possibility of allowing urban disciples to exercise leadership in their local church communities.

Of course, on the start of your SIAFU Chapter, you may only have a handful of members, perhaps not even enough members of the Chapter to account for all the Officers and support leaders! Be flexible and open to the Lord; do what you can to start, but be open to filling out these positions as God brings more members into your Chapter. We are confident that, with God's blessing and help, your Chapter will grow in number and strength, and this growth will more and more require good order, clear records, and open dialogue over all matters in the Chapter. Identifying, equipping, and releasing urban disciples for leadership is precisely what the SIAFU Network is about!

Please note: It is important to restate that these positions and the SIAFU Chapter itself are under the authority and blessing of the pastor or spiritual authority in a particular church or organization that is sponsoring the Chapter. *Under no circumstances can a Chapter operate without the pastor or spiritual authority's blessing (chaplain, director, etc.).* No Chapter can function on its own; it must be connected to a local assembly or organization whose pastor and spiritual authority has endorsed its work.

In summary, here are the key facts and principles regarding membership and leadership in a Chapter:

- Individuals join SIAFU Chapters by affirming their personal faith in Jesus Christ, their commitment to SIAFU's mission and vision and its rules, policies, and Statement of Faith, and agree to submit to the Chapter's Leadership Council.

- Candidate members should be publicly affirmed in a charge given to them by the President during a Chapter meeting, where they become official members of the Chapter (see Appendix for *SIAFU Member Charge*).

- All officers and leaders serve under the blessing and endorsement of the church pastor or ministry director.

- Officers and leaders are elected for one-year terms, by simple majority vote of the Chapter members.

- All activities, projects, and programs of any SIAFU Chapter must be subject to the approval of the pastor/ministry director of the sponsoring church or ministry.

Again, members of a SIAFU Chapter must be professing Christians, and Officers and Support Role leaders are to be selected annually by majority vote of the members present, with the pastor's or spiritual authority's blessing and imprimatur (endorsement).

PRESIDENT

The Chapter President serves at the behest of, as liaison of, and under the authority of the pastor/leader of the church and/or ministry. Essentially, the pastor/ministry leader should be regarded as an ex officio member of all SIAFU meetings, i.e., they can attend all meetings, whether planning or sponsored, of the SIAFU Chapter or its Leadership Council. The

President will call and chair the SIAFU Chapter Leadership Council and provide general communication to the pastor and the members of the Chapter about its ongoing business and operations.

The President is required to communicate with the pastor/ministry director regarding proposed projects of the Chapter, securing the pastor's blessing to proceed. S/he also should ensure that the Chapter conforms to the doctrine of the church, and to SIAFU Chapter guidelines. The President will preside over the Chapter meetings, opening and closing each meeting, and ensuring that the one-hour-and-fifteen-minute time limit for the meeting is held to consistently. S/he will open the meeting with a welcome of all Chapter attendees. The president will offer or select someone to provide the devotion for each Chapter meeting and will select the person who will lead the worship time for the week.

VICE PRESIDENT

Serves as assistant to the president and takes responsibility for the Chapter meetings in the president's absence. Also, the vice president should preside over Council meetings, when and if the president is absent. The VP role is to provide support for the President and ensure that the decisions of the President and affairs of the Chapter are carried out, both in terms of the Chapter meetings, as well as all other Chapter business. The Vice President should be able and ready to step into the President role, if and whenever necessary.

SECRETARY

The Secretary of the Chapter will manage the records, paperwork, and membership aspect of the Chapter. S/he will keep the list of all the official SIAFU Chapter members and provide reporting on membership, when called upon. The Secretary will keep record of Leadership Council meetings, providing the official minutes for review, and summarize conversations had within the meeting. S/he will note the decisions made and assignments given, and when called upon will communicate to Chapter members regarding Chapter business in between meetings, (e.g., changes in schedule or meeting locations, cancellations, etc.) S/he will also handle all communication with TUMI headquarters, such as questions, online testimonies, suggestions, and pictures.

TREASURER

The Treasurer of the Chapter is charged with managing and overseeing the finances and resources of the Chapter, including (but not limited to) collecting funds for specific events or projects, keeping track of Chapter expenses and funds, and reporting on finances of the Chapter to Chapter leadership, to Chapter members, and to church/ministry leaders. The Treasurer should be prepared to provide regular, detailed reports of the Chapter's financial status to its members.

HOST/HOSTESS

This role applies to each regular Chapter gathering. The Host/Hostess should ensure that the meeting room is clean and set up before each Chapter meeting; cleaned up afterward; trash taken out and room left in better shape than when meeting started. S/he should also coordinate snacks, set out meeting refreshments, and put away food afterward. Finally, the Host/Hostess should enlist the help of volunteers after the meeting to clean up and arrange the room as they found it.

SERVICE PROJECT COORDINATOR

This can be either a roving role, i.e., each service project can have a different Service Project Coordinator, or a Chapter can have a single Service Project Coordinator to coordinate all the projects for a given period of time. The Service Project Coordinator should research and select service projects for the Chapter. S/he should work with the Treasurer for necessary project funds and coordinate service project at the location(s) of project. S/he should also assign someone to take photos of project and get photos to the Vice President.

YOUR LEADERSHIP COUNCIL AGENDA TEMPLATE
HOW TO STRATEGIZE TOGETHER TO GROW YOUR CHAPTER

Meet regularly as a Chapter Council to keep track of Chapter business.
The Officers (president, vice president, secretary, and treasurer) of the Chapter should meet regularly (once each month, minimum) to plan out Chapter business, address ongoing issues, and review progress toward its goals. The more you can get together to prayerfully consider what is happening and what you believe God wants you to do, the better and more effective your Chapter will be.

The officers of the Chapter will be responsible to set together the strategic direction of your Chapter, to boil that vision down to practical goals, and then to communicate those goals to your Chapter members for the upcoming year. Once elected, set regular times to get together, consider old and new business, and to plan together your Chapter direction as you pursue what you believe God wants the Chapter to do in the next twelve months. Each officer meeting is important, so you should strive to be both efficient and clear on all matters you address. The following general order provides you with an adjustable agenda which you can modify to keep you on target as you consider both old and new business together as a council.

GENERAL ORDER FOR LEADERSHIP COUNCIL MEETING

1. President call the meeting to order and open with prayer

2. Biblical Devotional, selected person

3. Time to share personal updates, testimonies

Allow for Council members to update their personal situation. Each officer can share any prayer requests or special challenges they currently need prayer for.

4. Approval of minutes and discussion of any old business
   Minutes from previous meeting are read, discussed, and approved. Give opportunity to discuss any old or unresolved issues or business from previous meeting.

   a. Status of the Chapter's finances, membership, and relationship with the sponsoring church/organizations

   b. Review of last meeting's concerns, decisions, and assignments

   c. Review effectiveness of Chapter's previous service project (if necessary) and discuss ongoing status of pending projects

5. Review of Chapter current needs and new business

   a. Review and discuss Chapter calendar events, and make sure no conflicts exist for upcoming events and meetings

   b. Any pressing or new critical needs observed in the Chapter right now (each officer to address chapter needs/concerns they see)

   c. Brainstorm as a Council how observed needs might be met through the Chapter (or other parties). What are some things (goals) we would like to accomplish in this next year (what results do we want)?

   d. Determine what goals, if any, you as a Chapter will pursue in the coming months, and how, i.e., what service projects will we consider for the next months to address our Chapter's greatest needs and opportunities?

e. Status and update on project plans, and needs for the future

6. Review minutes of the Council meeting, including all decisions, dates, assignments, and projects discussed. Affirm notes and secure date of next Council meeting.

7. Adjourn Council meeting with prayer.

HOW TO ACCESS TUMI'S RESOURCES
EDIFYING AND EQUIPPING YOUR SIAFU CHAPTER MEMBERS

The following are representative of resources we have created for SIAFU and our satellites for equipping laborers for the work of the ministry. We are always creating additional tools to help strengthen the urban church, her members, and her leaders. Check our website frequently for the complete listing of all that is available (www.tumi.org/siafu).

The SIAFU Network Guidebook
This one-stop booklet provides all you need to establish your SIAFU chapter

SIAFU Chapter Meeting Guide
A handy resource for chapter leaders to organize their chapter meetings

The SIAFU Network Website (www.tumi.org/siafu)
SIAFU's online storehouse filled with numerous aids for your Chapter, with info to connect your Chapter to the entire network of SIAFU Chapters across the country (and around the world)

The SIAFU Chapter Resource Kit
A valuable and must-have toolbox for every SIAFU Chapter, which includes:

- One official, embossed SIAFU Certificate printed with your Chapter Name (for approved SIAFU Chapters)

- One additional *SIAFU Network Guidebook*

- Two *SIAFU Network Chapter Meeting Guides*

- One *Let God Arise! Prayer Booklet* with a pack of ten brochures

- Twenty SIAFU Network brochures

- One copy of the *Mo' Power* Spiritual Warfare Series CD (which contains a digital studio mixed version of the *SIAFU Chant*)

- One 24" x 36" SIAFU poster

Suggested Service Projects
A constantly updated list of potential service projects that your SIAFU Chapter can do to show Christ's love to your church and/or community

Listing of SIAFU Events and Conferences
SIAFU-sponsored events and conferences provide opportunities for worship, networking, service, and partnership among Chapters

Resources for Discipleship and Leadership

- *Fit to Represent: The Vision for Discipleship Seminar*: TUMI's attempt to raise up a new generation of qualified spiritual laborers who will catch the passion to invest in others for the sake of the Church and Christ's Kingdom

- *The Sacred Roots Follow-Up Curriculum*: a biblical and practical follow-up course for new and growing Christians in the city

- *Jesus Cropped from the Picture* (by Don Allsman): an insightful commentary on the problem of why Christians get bored and how to overcome it

- *Sacred Roots: A Primer on the Great Tradition*: an overview of the foundation of Christian faith and practice, and how we can renew our contemporary faith

- *Get Up and Go: Lessons in Freedom and the Power to Produce* (by Daniel Davis): a look at creative freedom through the lens of punk culture, and what it can teach disciples of Christ today on how to live free for Christ

- *Let God Arise! Prayer Booklet and Prayer Brochure*: a challenging prayer booklet issuing a call to people to intercede on behalf of the healing and transformation of the cities of America and the world

- *TUMI Art and Prints*: a wide array of beautiful and affordable Christian art available for purchase today

- *The Foundations for Ministry Series*: informative and inspiring Bible studies on various topics designed for personal and small group use

- *The Most Amazing Story Ever Told*: a booklet explaining the wonder and power of the Christian story for city Christians

- *Once Upon a Time*: brochure and poster of the entire Christian Story

THE SIAFU CHANT

124 bpm

                   Em

Verse 1:   We're unashamed (Without a tear),   we're unafraid (Without a fear)

                          C

We'll never quit (We holdin' ground),   we gonna stay (We hangin' 'round!)

               Am

All for one (And one for all)

                    B7

We're for the King (And for the call)

               Em

We hold the faith (We go before)

                    D   D on 4 downbeats

We shout and sing (We makin' war!)

                    Em

Chorus: Here we are, (We can't be dissed),   here we be, (We won't be missed)

                  C

Here we march, (We settin' out),   here we speak, (We all shout)

                Am

Here we fight, (We throwin' down)

            B7

Here we roll, (Around town)

               Em

Here we glide, (We on the move)

          D   D on 4 downbeats

Here we go, (SIAFU!)

                Em

Verse 2:   Honor bound (To do the right),   right on time (To stand and fight)

                  C

We stick around (In unity),   we seek to find (To set them free)

                    Am

We fight to win (To liberate)

               B7

We can't be beat (We dedicate)

                Em

We're going in (On full attack)

                  D   D on 4 downbeats

We won't retreat (We'll take it back!)

(to Chorus)

                Em

End: Here we are, SIAFU! Here we are, SIAFU!

Here we are, SIAFU! Here we are, SIAFU!

SIAFU!

SIAFU Membership Charge

Ask new SIAFU members to come forward and stand, facing the President of the Chapter, the one who serves as the commissioner on behalf of the Chapter.

Commissioner

In the presence of the Lord, and in the company of these fellow SIAFU members, we acknowledge you all standing here as new members of our fellowship, the SIAFU Chapter of [church or organization name]. On the basis of your profession of faith in Christ Jesus as your personal Lord and Savior, and by virtue of your voluntary commitment to our movement, we welcome you into our Chapter, upon your answer of the following questions:

As a member of [Church or Organization Name] SIAFU Chapter, will you strive through the Spirit's leading to grow in grace and in the knowledge of Jesus Christ?

[Members say, "I will."]

Will you gather regularly and faithfully in your own chosen church family, and actively participate in your church's body life, fellowship, and service together?

[Members say, "I will."]

Will you allow the Lord to faithfully use your life and gifts to build up the members of this Chapter, as the Lord gives you the strength and opportunity?

[Members say, "I will."]

Will you generously support the Chapter's life and ministry together, giving time, money, and effort to see it advance the Kingdom here in this place?

[Members say, "I will."]

Will you pray for your unsaved friends, relatives, neighbors, and associates to become Christ's disciples, and do what you can to help them become followers of Jesus, as God leads?

[MEMBERS SAY, "I WILL."]

Will you strive to build up your fellow SIAFU members, and support and be responsive to the Chapter's leadership council?

[MEMBERS SAY, "I WILL."]

In light of your profession of faith in Jesus, and public commitment to the Chapter's vision and aims, we welcome you into our family, to share in all the privileges, responsibilities, and challenges of the SIAFU Network, as we strive to follow Christ together.

Let us pray.

[COMMISSIONER PRAYS TO THE LORD]

Come, brothers (or sisters), let's greet these new members of our [Church or Organization Name] SIAFU Chapter family!

DEVELOPING EFFECTIVE SERVICE PROJECT GROUPS
HELPING YOUR CHAPTER ORGANIZE AROUND BURDEN-DRIVEN SERVICE PROJECTS
Rev. Dr. Don L. Davis

This paper is an adaptation of an article written for an inner-city church plant which organized its witness around burden-centered cell groups. I have adapted its language from those of cell groups to those of service project teams. By organizing your service projects around the shared burdens and visions of your members, you will be able to accomplish many exciting, practical projects which meet the real needs of others in your community. Each of these initiatives, whether they focus on providing service to others or on outreach to unsaved friends and neighbors, can be organized around particular teams of Chapter members who strive to represent the Chapter in their works of service.

SIAFU Chapters can use service project groups to help their members identify, commit, and organize around specific problems they want to address or particular burdens they possess. As you plan out your service projects for your Chapter, you should consult this article to find out specifically how you can encourage your members to be sensitive to their own burdens for others, and how to turn those burdens into practical service projects that meet real needs where you live.

As you organize your Chapter service projects, you may elect to host more than a single project at any given time. Based on the money, interest, and involvement of your members, you may plan several projects to run alongside each other simultaneously. Also, you might choose to divide different members into groups to work on separate projects at different times. This idea of planning multiple service projects allows you to tap into the different interests your members may have. You can easily encourage your members to serve based on their burdens and opportunities and give those members the chance to work together based on their shared interest.

Whether or not you choose to occasionally divide your members up into different service teams or work together as a single Chapter on a project, you will find the insights in the article helpful for your thinking and planning. Whatever you elect to do – working together as a single Chapter on a project or dividing your members up into teams to work on different projects – count on Christ to guide you as you learn to do good works together. Be open to God, and let the Spirit lead you as you as a Chapter combine your time and talent together to make a practical difference in your community.

The following is taken from World Impact's paper on planting churches cross-culturally:

> The initial cell groups take on different characteristics according to the needs and distinctives of the target group. Bible study groups study the Word of God corporately and develop new relationships in the community. Contact groups are action-oriented, focusing on evangelization through special events such as concerts or other outreach activities. Forum groups discuss issues of community interest or concern, gaining biblical insights and awakening people's understanding of a Christian world view. Other groups could be created based on an understanding of the gifts, personalities and needs of the participants. Regardless of the particular accent, each type of group should evidence the five activities mentioned in Acts 2.41-47: study, fellowship, worship, stewardship and witness.

The most viable form of service project organization is that which flows out of the burden of our SIAFU Chapter members, the kind that encourages its members to flesh out in practical Christian service their shared commitment to that burden.

DEFINITION OF "BURDEN"

"An interest, desire, passion, or commitment to address a specific need or situation, to do good works, to make a difference, or to touch the life of some person or group with the love and gospel of Christ."

1. They deal with ministering to others (have to do with exercising one's gifts for the good of the body and the community).

2. They address needs which are felt, observed, or are brought to the attention of its members.

3. They give direction, life, and purpose to the service project team.

GENERAL FACTS ABOUT BURDENS AND SERVICE GROUPS IN THE BODY

1. God gives burdens to his people to match their gifts and their calling.

2. Burdens usually begin with the felt needs of the participants to build up themselves in Christ, but naturally grow to meeting the needs of others.

3. Burdens involve not just our understanding, but our heart desires, our emotions, and those deep concerns which move us to compassion and to action.

4. Burdens may be developed through prayer, involvement and study.

5. People possess different burdens in varying degrees.

    a. Some may last only for a period of time.

    b. Some may organize to address a specific issue or concern.

    c. Some may evolve into separate ministries or outreaches.

    d. Some may cross-pollinate with others, forming new combinations of groups.

BENEFITS OF BURDEN-ORIENTED GROUPS

A number of clear benefits arise from organizing our cell life around the particular burdens of the members to edify and serve. Burdens may be developed through prayer, involvement, and study.

1. We affirm the usefulness and importance of each Chapter member's heart concerns.

2. We allow for the freedom of the Spirit to raise up new burdens, visions, and opportunities in the midst of our Chapter.

3. We encourage each person to take their interests, desires, and intuitions seriously in regards to what they believe God is calling them to do.

4. We affirm the biblical truth that every Christian has gifts and a calling, and that we can be united in our use of different gifts, roles, and responsibilities in the body.

5. We maximize the potential we have for everyone to find a place of belonging and ministry outreach in our body.

6. We can easily organize the service projects of our Chapter around the creative passions of our members, rather than arbitrarily around age characteristics, marital status, or some other criteria.

7. We multiply our ability to meet needs both within our body and in our community by encouraging all members to find outlets for the burdens and desires they have for ministry and support.

8. We build Christian community among our Chapter members by finding through our projects a concrete outlet for their service, witness and ministry.

9. We give opportunity for people with unique and different burdens to attempt to generate interest and support for their activities and concerns.

10. We allow the flow of our members' own heart concerns to dictate the outreach of our church and the expenditure of our resources.

11. We safeguard ourselves against building institutional traditions that no longer grow from the passions and commitments of the members themselves.

CAUTIONS AND QUESTIONS ABOUT BURDEN-DRIVEN MINISTRY

Several possible problems or issues may be raised about organizing one's life together around the burdens of its members. We affirm the usefulness/significance of each body member's heart concerns.

1. *Do you organize around each individual member's burdens, even if only one or two share that particular concern?*

   Answer: It is reasonable to assume that not every burden will be given outlet in a body with limited resources, monies, and people. No church has unlimited resources or people; each must choose what it can and cannot support. Members should be encouraged to articulate their concerns. But practically some burdens might have to be prioritized, or members may have to participate in groups which share a similar (not identical) burden. In addition, some people are moved in their heart to become involved in ministries which lie outside their training, qualifications, and resources. While we must strive to provide opportunity for all to pursue their burdens, we also should be good stewards of God's resources to make our greatest impact. We have limited time and resources; we will have to decide which projects we can do, and when we can do them. We must make hard decisions, and not spread our efforts around so broadly that we wind up being ineffective at anything. Seek God, and move forward with what you believe God wants you to do.

2. *What if people have a burden for the wrong thing?*

   Answer: Since we are committed to the Word of God, all proposed concerns will necessarily have to pass the test of being consistent with the revealed heart of God shown most clearly in the life and ministry of Jesus Christ.

3. *How do you maintain unity in a church which organizes itself around such different burdens, emphases, and concerns?*

   Answer: Rather than undercutting unity, such a practice affirms the biblical principle of the equality, unity, and diversity of the members of the church. The SIAFU Network is anchored in churches and organizations where Christians are considered equal in importance and stature in the church. Our Chapters are diverse by virtue of the burdens, gifts, and callings of the many members within them. We build unity among our Chapter members as we affirm our single desire to glorify God by advancing the Kingdom and building up the body of Christ through its worship, works, and witness. A Chapter project team organized around a burden for ministry should wholeheartedly commit itself to the vision and mission of the entire Chapter and the church-at-large, not seeking to divide the Chapter or church, but to express its service as a representative of the Chapter itself.

4. *Isn't there a chance of undue favoritism or a "bandwagon" spirit – won't some teams prosper and grow, while others, equally valid, shrink and even die?*

   Answer: The life of a service group is a dynamic reality; no one can predict if the members of a church will coalesce around a particular burden or not, or whether God will give the same burden of ministry to a large number of people or not. The Spirit should be given freedom to work with the members to place on their hearts differing kinds of issues, concerns, or needs. As time goes on, and as members seek the Lord and leaders facilitate this process, God will give you insight into what needs you can and should meet. Some projects may be beyond both your abilities and capacities. Some you may even try to do, even though you can't do everything you might like to do. If God is given the greatest latitude to speak and lead the church in new and unforeseen ways, different kinds of ministries will emerge, in different sizes and emphasis, for different periods of time. The key will always be your ability to listen to the Spirit and your willingness to respond together to his prompting. Count on God leading you step by step, and be bold to meet the needs you can.

How to Develop a Burden-Oriented Service Group

Below are some ideas regarding how such burden-oriented groups might start. These are only suggestions; these groups may be organized in a number of different ways for different purposes.

1. Develop some mechanism for identifying the different concerns, issues, needs, and opportunities the members of the body are interested in addressing, studying, or meeting.

2. Gather the people together who share a common burden, seeking to match the interests as closely as possible.

3. Encourage the group to meet together to discern what in particular they desire to accomplish, and how that relates to the overall mission of the church.

4. The group should be encouraged to think through practically the nature of their burden and their particular field of interest, and how it relates to the Chapter's mission and vision as a whole.

   a. This will enable them to clarify their purpose as a service group.

   b. This can be used to communicate to others who may be interested in joining.

   c. This may be used to evaluate the effectiveness of the group's efforts as it strives to fulfill its purpose.

5. Once the service group is clear on its mission, the group might want to brainstorm different goal possibilities which address specifically what the group wants to do in its upcoming service project.

6. After prayer and discussion, select from the group of possibilities some specific goals you intend to accomplish, writing them down, making certain that your goal statements are measurable and attainable.

7. Each goal should be prayerfully considered and strategically planned, detailing what must be done as the goal is pursued. Four questions may help in this process:

   a. What precisely do we hope to accomplish?

   b. When exactly or how frequently do we want to do it?

   c. What person(s) are needed to make the plan a reality?

   d. What resources do we need to acquire, and when, to accomplish our goal?

8. Set dates, give assignments, and make preparation to carry out your service project. Make sure that you communicate with the Project Coordinator for the Chapter regularly, and keep all team members informed of any changes to the plan as things develop.

9. Follow through on your service project as a team, getting as much accomplished as you possibly can within the time available. Emphasize the need to be punctual on site, to work hard and efficiently together throughout the entire project, and make sure that you finish well, cleaning up all things and setting things in place, once you have completed your work.

10. After the project, make sure that the team meets together soon afterwards to evaluate the success of the time and brainstorm ways on what could have been done differently in order to make the project even more efficient and successful. Also, make sure that you provide a report to the Chapter on what results your efforts made, and how the project fulfilled your Chapter's local vision.

11. Finally, make certain that you file any planning papers or materials about this project somewhere handy for the Chapter's retrieval. All the insight you obtain from hosting this project may prove valuable, if another service project team decides to do a similar activity or event some time in the future.

THE SOJOURNER'S QUEST
Don L. Davis

Sojourning as pilgrims on a quest to see the Great King
To share the same core, the same hope, the same dream

Walking shoulder-to-shoulder, every burden we bear
With patient conviction, with warmth and great care

In friendship with Christ, our Glory and Crown
That in Him alone our real joy would be found

To see with new eyes ev'ry single soul's worth
To cherish the least of these above all else on earth

To burn with deep longing that His praises might flow
And through our sweet unity His beauty might show

Yes, this is our goal, our glory, our aim
That Christ might be seen on this earth once again

That His kingdom and glory would be powerfully known
That more of His likeness through us might be shown

That for the sake of our friends we would lay down our lives
That His fruit might be borne, and His grace multiplied

That by sharing in common our lights would so shine
That the world might be drawn to Him, one heart at a time

And every broken vessel, however humble or meek
Might taste our Lord's mercies, be healed, and set free

We count now as dung all this world's sweetest pleasures
We press toward the goal for the Kingdom's true treasures

We invite you to join us in our glorious quest
To sojourn with us gladly to His coronation, as guest

We give all that we are and we have to one thing –
To dine soon at His banquet before Christ the Great King

WORLD IMPACT

TRANSFORMING COMMUNITIES TOGETHER

World Impact, Inc., TUMI's parent ministry, is an interdenominational missions organization committed to facilitating church-planting movements by evangelizing, equipping, and empowering the unchurched urban poor.

Evangelism: *Everything we say and do that reveals the love of God to our neighbors.*

Equipping: *Training urban disciples to live a healthy Christian life and to make new disciples.*

Empowerment: *Indigenously led church-based ministries transforming communities together.*

Purpose Statement
Our Purpose is to honor and glorify God and delight in Him among the unchurched urban poor by knowing God and making Him known.

Mission Statement
As a Christian missions organization, we are committed to facilitating church planting movements by evangelizing, equipping, and empowering America's urban poor.

Vision Statement
Our vision is to recruit, empower, and release urban leaders who will plant churches and launch indigenous church planting movements.

Global Ends Statement
The empowered urban poor advancing God's Kingdom in every city through the local church.

FOUR FOCUS AREAS (WITH THEIR INITIATIVES):

1. PLANTING HEALTHY URBAN CHURCHES *Target the unchurched and under-resourced individuals in urban communities* * Crowns of Beauty – World Impact Church Planting Movement * Evangel – Church Planting School	**2. DEVELOPING MISSIONAL PARTNERSHIPS** *Forming Kingdom-minded relationships that collaboratively love, serve, and engage under-resourced communities* * Urban Church Associations * The Bridge – Cross-cultural, missional engagements with suburban churches * The Zion Project – Partnerships with urban churches
3. RESOURCING URBAN LEADERS *Equipping indigenous church leaders to shepherd the people of God within their own communities* * World Impact Associates – Indigenous leaders hired to implement our initiatives * Conferences and Events – Camps, TUMI Summit, Church Plant School, and city festivals * TUMI Satellites	**4. DEMONSTRATING COMPASSION AND JUSTICE** *Mobilizing local churches to be outposts of the Kingdom of God. These outposts demonstrate in tangible ways the compassion and justice to under-resourced urban communities.* * SIAFU Chapters * SIAFU Leadership Homes (I2I) * Modeling Ministries

TUMI
FACT SHEET

The Urban Ministry Institute
3701 East 13th Street | Wichita, Kansas 67208
Email: contactus@tumi.org | Tel: 316.681.1317 | www.tumi.org

a ministry of
WORLD IMPACT
TRANSFORMING COMMUNITIES TOGETHER

Our Identity

The Urban Ministry Institute (TUMI) is the training arm of World Impact, an interdenominational missions organization committed to facilitating church-planting movements by evangelizing, equipping, and empowering the unchurched urban poor. TUMI's role in that vision is to equip leaders for the urban church, especially among the poor, in order to advance the Kingdom of God.

Our Mission

Dedicated to equipping leaders and empowering movements, our focus is clear: **Resourcing the Great Commission.** We provide innovative resources, consultations, and events to enable churches and organizations to do effective ministry among the lost, especially among the poor, from evangelism, discipleship, church planting, and leadership development.

Our History

In 2015 TUMI celebrated its twentieth year of operation. A brief overview of our history reveals our dedication to equipping qualified spiritual laborers among the poor:

1995

TUMI founded by Dr. Don Davis
Since July of 1995 we have hosted hundreds of courses locally at our Hope School of Ministry as well as nationally in conjunction with other ministries or organizations.

Capstone is a 16-module training program providing seminary-level instruction specifically designed for emerging leaders to gain expertise in the historic orthodox faith and the most essential knowledge and skill learning needed for effective urban ministry and church leadership.

2000

Began *Let God Arise! Prayer Movement*
This movement began with our belief that only God can change the city. www.letgodarise.com

Established TUMI Satellite Program
TUMI's Satellite Program allows churches, denominations, and other Christian ministries to equip their own leaders affordably, right where they are.

Held first *Evangel School for Urban Church Planting*
Over the years we have trained dozens of church plant teams for city work. In 2015 we hosted our first Dean Training for the Evangel School, enabling others to sponsor their own church plant school training.

Ten years in the making, Capstone includes four courses in each of four ministry areas: Biblical Studies, Theology and Ethics, Christian Ministry, Urban Mission (totaling 16 modules, 10,000+ pages of text, 64 hours of video, 41 required textbooks). Each module contains a Mentor's Guide, a student workbook, and DVD teaching segments.

2005

Capstone Curriculum completed

Capstone is currently available in English and Spanish. Romanian, Telugu, Arabic, and Hindi translations are in the works.

2006

Received grant to expand satellite network
This grant allowed us to grow from 15 satellites to more than 150.

2008

Began formal partnership with Prison Fellowship
This strategic partnership allowed us to launch a pilot program to bring TUMI from a handful of prisons to 32 California state prisons. We are now in 66 prisons and county or local jails.

This national association of chapters is anchored in local urban churches and ministries dedicated to the city. SIAFU chapters are designed to help identify, equip, and release spiritually qualified servant leaders to reach and transform America's neediest, unreached communities.

2013

Established *The SIAFU Network*

2014

Developed *Fight the Good Fight of Faith*
This book is a follow-up curriculum/pre-Capstone course that is being used by pastors and leaders to disciple new believers.

Our Statistics (as of August, 2016)

- 245 satellites
  (69 sites offer training in prisons and/or jails)
- 17 countries
  (US, Mexico, El Salvador, Romania, Ghana, Liberia, Nigeria, Kenya, India, Honduras, Spain, South Africa, Cuba, Tanzania, Cameroon, Guatemala, and Ecuador)
- 2,787 students
  (317 international students; 1,229 incarcerated students)
- 564 graduates
- 18 SIAFU chapters

Our Academic Connections

Although TUMI maintains a voluntary unaccredited status (in order to provide maximum access for urban leaders who may not qualify for traditional academic training) we have formed partnerships with several schools, universities, and seminaries which offer our graduates credit toward the completion of their own degree programs, including:

- Tabor College
- Lancaster Bible College
- Nyack College
- Fuller Theological Seminary
- City Vision University

We are a member of the *Association of Biblical Higher Education's* non-accredited class of institutions, recognized for our voluntary non-accreditation status, in order that we might provide maximum access of seminary-level training to non-traditional students who otherwise would not qualify for such instruction.

Our Partnerships

We currently partner with different denominations, ministries, and organizations to help establish programming and infrastructure to provide seminary-level training for their pastors and ministry leaders including:

- Church of God in Christ
- Evangelical Free Church of America
- Charismatic Episcopal Church
- Prison Fellowship
- Urban Ministries, Inc.
- Evangelical Covenant Church of America
- Awana Lifeline

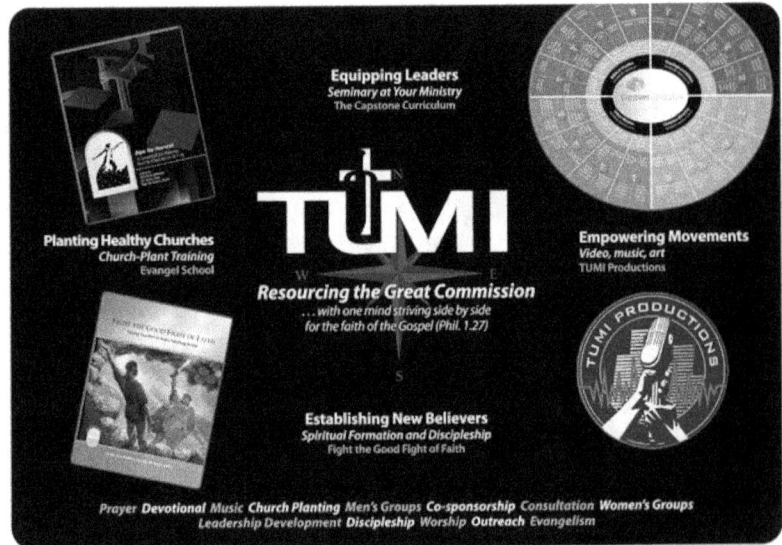

equipping leaders. empowering movements.

Our Commitment to the Future

To meet the ever-growing global demand for solid biblical training that is affordable, accessible, and culturally relevant for the poor, TUMI has been charged with a vision to retool our operations for an even greater capacity. Our goal is to train 100,000 students with our *Fight the Good Fight of Faith* discipleship resource, equip 10,000 leaders in Capstone, expand to 820 satellites, and penetrate into 40 countries and 12 languages by 2021, World Impact's 50th anniversary year.

In order to resource this worthy vision we will translate *Fight the Good Fight of Faith* into 20 languages and *The Capstone Curriculum* into 10 additional languages.

The Urban Ministry Institute

3701 East 13th Street | Wichita, Kansas 67208
Email: contactus@tumi.org | Tel: 316.681.1317 | www.tumi.org

a ministry of

THE URBAN MINISTRY INSTITUTE
HELPING CHAPTERS TO REDISCOVER VITAL SPIRITUALITY!
Rev. Dr. Don L. Davis

We believe that in order to renew our personal and corporate walks in the contemporary church we must simply return and rediscover our Sacred Roots, i.e., the core beliefs, practices, and commitments of the Christian faith. These roots are neither sectarian nor provincial, but are rather cherished and recognized by all believers everywhere, at all times, and by everyone. Paul exhorted the Thessalonians, "So then, brothers, stand firm and hold to the traditions that you were taught by us, either by our spoken word or by our letter" (2 Thess. 2.15). Our Sacred Roots necessarily suggest that all who believe (wherever and whenever they have lived) affirm their common rootedness in the saving work of God, the same Lord who created, covenanted with Israel, was incarnate in Christ, and is being witnessed to by his people, the Church.

JESUS CROPPED FROM THE PICTURE:
WHY CHRISTIANS GET BORED AND HOW TO
RESTORE THEM TO VIBRANT FAITH, REV. DON ALLSMAN

Why are many churches shrinking? Why are so many Christians bored? Could it be that the well-meaning attempt to simplify the gospel message for contemporary culture has produced churches full of discouraged people secretly longing for something more? Jesus Cropped from the Picture describes this phenomenon and proposes a return to our sacred roots as a guard against spiritual lethargy and a way to enhance spiritual vibrancy.

SACRED ROOTS: A PRIMER ON RETRIEVING
THE GREAT TRADITION, DR. DON L. DAVIS

The Christian Faith is anchored on the person and work of Jesus of Nazareth, the Christ, whose incarnation, crucifixion, and resurrection forever changed the world. Between the years 100 and 500 C.E. those who believed in him grew from a small persecuted minority to a strong aggressive movement reaching far beyond the bounds of the Roman empire. The roots this era produced gave us our canon (the Scriptures), our worship, and our conviction (the major creeds of the Church, and the central tenets of the Faith, especially regarding the doctrine of the Trinity and Christ). This book suggests how we can renew our contemporary faith again, by rediscovering these roots, our Sacred Roots, by retrieving the Great Tradition of the Church that launched the Christian revolution.

PARTICIPATING IN URBAN CHURCH PLANTING MOVEMENTS

If you are interested in more of Dr. Davis's ideas on how to facilitate or participate in urban church planting movements and how you can help sustain them through retrieving the Great Tradition, be sure to get your own copies of the following three *Foundations for Ministry Series* courses. These three courses are central to discussing what we understand the focus of urban mission to be, both in terms of the aim of it (i.e., to multiply churches rapidly among the urban poor), and the substance of it (i.e., retrieving and expressing The Great Tradition with churches that contextualize it).

WINNING THE WORLD:
FACILITATING URBAN CHURCH PLANTING MOVEMENTS

At a time when our definitions of the Church have become more and more individualized, this study analyzes church plant and growth theories as they relate to the more communal Nicene-based marks of church life. Using these marks as the basis for a more biblical view of the Church, this study discusses and investigates the connection between church planting, world evangelization, church growth, leadership development, and urban mission. It clearly identifies the underlying principles which have contributed to the explosive multiplication of churches in places like India, Latin America, and China, and proposes the possibility of similar movements of revival, renewal, and reproduction among the poor in American cities. This course lays the foundation for the necessary principles underlying key elements of a Church Planting Movement and what it would take to facilitate and participate in one [workbook and MP3 audio – visit *www.tumi.org/foundations*].

CHURCH MATTERS:
RETRIEVING THE GREAT TRADITION

At a time of turbulence and dramatic change in society and uneasiness and compromise in the Church, it is critical for believers to retain a sense of the history of the body of Christ. What is needed today is a sense of perspective, i.e., coming to view and understand current events through the lens of God's working through the Church through the ages. Armed with a sense of history, we will be both encouraged and challenged that our current situation is neither unique nor unresolvable. Through the great movements of the Church, the Holy Spirit has shown that even in the face of schism, compromise, difficulty, and persecution, the people of God can learn, grow, and fulfill God's plan for them. This course shows that you can rediscover the power of the living biblical tradition of the Church, anchored in the person and work of Jesus Christ, and how essential it is to ground our Church Planting on something larger than us. Throughout its history, the Church has proven that God's unique plan can unfold even in the face of schism and persecution. Such wisdom is critical to renew and revive the urban church today [workbook and MP3 audio – visit *www.tumi.org/foundations*].

MARKING TIME:
FORMING SPIRITUALITY THROUGH THE CHRISTIAN YEAR

In this course, we explore the origins and meaning of the Christian Year and how it represents the profound yet simple remembrance and re-enactment of the life of Christ in real time during the calendar year. Beginning with an overview of the Bible's teaching in connection to time and history, this course explores the dominant view of the atonement, Christus Victor, which reigned in the ancient Church for a thousand years. We look at how this dynamic vision of Jesus' victory over sin and death was captured in the worship of the Church in the Church Year. This course, then, lays out the argument and rationale for embracing the Church Year as a structure that enables us to enhance spiritual formation in the urban church setting [workbook and MP3 audio – visit *www.tumi.org/foundations*].

EVANGEL SCHOOL OF URBAN CHURCH PLANTING

For over twenty years World Impact and The Urban Ministry Institute have been equipping church planters working among the urban poor in the United States and around the world. Thousands of urban church leaders have received church plant training during this time and more than 150 church plants have been commissioned in partnership with local churches, associations, and denominations.

World Impact and The Urban Ministry Institute (TUMI) are looking for partners who are called to plant new churches among the poor. During the next six years World Impact and TUMI hope to see at least 300 new churches planted in America's inner cities. The *Evangel School of Urban Church Planting* provides a tool for urban churches, denominations, and mission agencies to host a contextualized church plant school in their city or region for those God has called to plant churches among the urban poor.

While the original Evangel School of Urban Church Planting was held in 2000, the year 2015 was the first time that TUMI officially certified other groups to run Evangel Church Planting Schools. In order to host an Evangel School, it is necessary for each potential church plant school to send at least two deans for certification to an Evangel Dean Training. Visit www.tumi.org/evangel for more information.

WORLD IMPACT'S AFFIRMATION OF FAITH

As a ministry of *World Impact, The Urban Ministry Institute* unequivocally endorses *World Impact's* Affirmation of Faith statement expressing our allegiance to the orthodox faith.

- There is one living and true God, infinitely perfect in glory, wisdom, holiness, justice, power and love, one in His essence but eternally existing in three persons: God the Father, God the Son and God the Holy Spirit. God sovereignly created the world out of nothing, so that His creation, while wholly dependent upon Him, neither comprises part of God, nor conditions His essential perfection.

- The books which form the canon of the Old and New Testaments are verbally inspired by God, inerrant in the original writings, the only infallible rule of faith and practice.

- God created man in His own image, in a state of original righteousness, from which humankind subsequently fell by a voluntary revolt, and consequently is guilty, inherently corrupt and subject to divine wrath.

- Jesus Christ, the eternal Son, became man without ceasing to be God by uniting to His divine nature a true human nature in His incarnation, and so continues to be both God and man, in two distinct natures and one person, forever. He was conceived by the Holy Spirit, born of the virgin Mary, exhibited His deity by manifold miracles, fulfilled the requirements of the Law by His sinless life, shed His blood as a vicarious and propitiatory atonement for humankind's sin, was resurrected from the dead in the same body, now glorified. He ascended into heaven and now intercedes in glory for His redeemed as our great high priest and advocate, and as the Head of the Church and Lord of the individual believer.

- The Holy Spirit convicts the world of sin, righteousness and judgment, through the ministry of regeneration and sanctification applies salvation and places believers into the Church, guides and comforts God's children, indwells, directs, gifts and empowers the Church in godly living and service in order to fulfill the Great Commission, and seals and keeps the believer until Christ returns.

- Every person, regardless of race or rank, who receives the Lord Jesus Christ by faith is born into the family of God and receives eternal life. This occurs solely because of the grace of God and has no ground in human merit.

- The Holy Church is the one institution specifically ordained of God to function in the furthering of the Kingdom until Christ comes again. It consists of all those regenerated by the Spirit of God, in mystical union and communion both with Christ, the head of the Body, and with fellow-believers. Neighborhood congregations are the local manifestation of the Church universal. In obedience to the command of Christ, these congregations preach the Word of God, equip God's people for the work of ministry, and administer the Lord's Supper and Baptism.

- The Lord Jesus Christ will return bodily, visibly and personally to receive His own, to conform believers to His own image and to establish His millennial kingdom. He will judge the quick and the dead and will effect a final separation of the redeemed and the lost, assigning unbelievers to eternal punishment and believers to eternal glory, enjoying conscious fellowship with Him.

- Humankind's chief end in life is to honor and glorify Almighty God. Personal salvation is a means to this end.

www.ingramcontent.com/pod-product-compliance
Lightning Source LLC
Chambersburg PA
CBHW081641040426

42449CB00015B/3410